Resist the Devil

A Pastoral Guide to Deliverance Prayer

Charles W. Harris, C.S.C.

Greenlawn Press

Library of Congress number 88-083043

ISBN 0-937779-07-5

Second printing

Printed in the United States of America

CONTENTS

ACKNOWLEDGMENTS

Numerous people have assisted in the production of this book. Their helpful insights, concerns and professional assistance are deeply and gratefully acknowledged. A special word of thanks is owed to Jill Boughton, for her dedicated editorial work, to Mary Frances Sparrow and Kay TePas for their assiduous research in following up references, to Janice Hanstad for typing up the entire manuscript in its first form, and to other fellow members of the People of Praise who shared their wisdom and discernment as this book developed.

INTRODUCTION

Kevin M. Ranaghan

The orthodox Christian tradition affirms the existence of the devil and of evil spirits. That same tradition also holds that Christians can call on divine assistance and power in combatting and defeating evil spirits and their influence. In a day when many religious writers state that the devil does not exist, it is refreshing to acknowledge Father Harris's book as a welcome addition to the literature of Christian pastoral concern regarding the influence of evil spirits on human beings.

Wise Christians know that dealing with the desires of the flesh and the attractions of the world is only part of their struggle to follow the Lord Jesus. Confronting the devil and rejecting him and his works are also essential matters in the spiritual life, and Father Harris has called upon his extensive study and practical experience to provide us with a modern and solidly founded approach to prayers for deliverance. Many people are looking for precisely this kind of help—whether as pastors or as those seeking pastoral guidance—and Father Harris's approach will provide the understanding and the help which so many are seeking.

After ordination in the Congregation of Holy Cross in 1943, he served as a university teacher of physics and administrator. During this period he also became deeply involved with a variety of renewal movements which have characterized the Catholic Church in the last third of this century. He was actively involved as a leader in the *Cursillo* movement from its earliest days in this country. He subsequently developed the Antioch Weekend, a university-based adaptation of the *Cursillo*. He was an early leader in the charismatic renewal and in the formation of charismatic communities, and a beloved leader in a charismatic community called the People of Praise.

In all these environments he served as pastor, spiritual director and counsellor. His grace and wisdom bore wonderful fruit. He died in 1988, as preparations for this book were entering their final stages, and has passed the "finish line" with his eyes looking steadfastly at his Lord, Jesus.

More important for the concerns of this book, he was for a number of years an authorized exorcist in the Archdiocese of Portland (Oregon). His experience in this role as well as his broad priestly and pastoral experience placed him in a remarkable position to write this book.

In these pages he accomplishes a number of purposes which, taken together, provide both a theological understanding and a practical guide for the discerning of evil spirits and for praying with people for deliverance from them. He draws from Scripture, the church Fathers and contemporary church teaching to characterize the strategies and operations of the devil. He does so in the context of the Christian belief that Satan has been conquered by Christ and that Christ's victory needs to be effectively applied and appropriated.

He welcomes the genuine insights of psychotherapy and the allied disciplines, which are of assistance in distinguishing between afflictions which are psychological in origin and those which are demonic.

To all this he adds a presentation of the seven capital sins, which in and of itself would make the book worthwhile. Father Harris shows that an adequate understanding of these capital vices is necessary in order to form right judgments about many spiritual difficulties the Christian encounters.

This is, in sum, a book about discernment, about making well-informed judgments, about using the gifts of the Holy Spirit in combatting the devil. In the end, Father Harris presents a simple method for ordinary Christians to use in small-group prayer for deliverance. He cautions against the excesses of large-scale deliverance ministries and steers clear of unauthorized and irresponsible exorcists. Instead, he offers a calm, well-balanced and well-informed method of deliverance prayer which he has used widely and found to be extremely effective.

This book can be seen as a response to the call of Pope Paul VI for further investigation into this area. It makes a genuine contribution to Catholics and all Christians who seek to overcome the flesh and the devil. It makes, indeed, a significant contribution to the ongoing pastoral research and practice of the church.

Author's Note

Many speakers and writers use the terms "exorcism" and "deliverance" interchangeably, while others use the terms to distinguish "formal" from "informal" prayers. Still others place the need for exorcism at the extreme edge of demonic interference (possession), with the need for deliverance only in cases of moderate harassment (obsession) by evil spirits. Some consider exorcism to be a command addressed to the demons, while deliverance is a prayer addressed to God. In this book, these terms have not been used as a vocabulary for making such distinctions.

Resist the Devil

1. THE TESTIMONY OF SCRIPTURE

Evil is a constant torment for the human race, and the problem of isolating and dealing with its source is both an individual and a universal concern. We constantly struggle with evil and where it comes from. In fact, though, only since the coming of Christ has the human race achieved some clarity about Satan—the source of all evil—and about the victory which is available to us as members of Christ's body, the church.

Throughout history, we find religious men and women unable to understand or to combat the evil they saw within themselves and in the world around them. For many religions, good and evil are not distinct; they are fused in an impersonal fate or chance. What happens is what happens, and the individual in harmony with the universe simply resigns himself to the way things are.

Nevertheless, human beings find it difficult to refrain from making moral judgments, judgments about good and evil. Some things are good, others evil. While people may not be able to come to universal agreement on which is which, they are usually not willing to say it makes no difference. Nor can a philosophy based on fate or chance easily dismiss the experience of free choice. Individuals not only distinguish good from evil but also choose between them, sometimes choosing what they see as good, sometimes evil.

Some primitive religions attempt to account for the human experience of good and evil in a different way. For them, good spiritual beings (gods) are in continual conflict with evil spiritual beings (demons). Gods originate goodness and protect their friends. Demons cause evil and punish those who fail to appease them. Primitive religions usually see these beings as equal in power.

Jewish thought, in turn, also seeks an explanation for evil in the world. The realm of nature is in disorder; so are social and spiritual relations. These contradict the goodness of the created order, and

1

they cannot be attributed to the God who reveals himself as both omnipotent and entirely good. What, then, is the origin of this evil which seems to antedate and exceed the scope of human sinfulness? In the Jewish understanding the origin of earthly evil lies in the rebellion of a heavenly being. This being used his freedom to reject God's invitation to be a servant creature; he tried instead to set himself up as God. St. Paul in 2 Thessalonians 2:3-4 calls this rebellious angel the "son of perdition, who opposes and exalts himself against every so-called god or object of worship, so that he takes his seat in the temple of God, proclaiming himself to be God." Unlike the demons of pagan religions, the devil remains subject to Almighty God.

In the 12th century, the Albigensians revived Manichaeism. This dualistic heresy acknowledged two independent sources of creation and of power, God and the devil: God creating all good, the devil all evil, and the two continually struggling to master mankind. In response to this heresy, the Fourth Lateran Council said: "We firmly believe and profess without qualification" that the Three Divine Persons "are the one and only principle of all things— Creator of all things visible and invisible.... For the devil and other demons were created by God good according to their nature, but they made themselves evil by their own doing. As for man, his sin was at the prompting of the devil."

References to Satan and evil spirits can be found in various parts of the Old Testament,[1] but there the theme is more rare and more subtle than in the Gospels. This does not mean that the concept of Satan is a late development; the account in Genesis 3 belongs to the oldest tradition in the Bible, and the material in the prologue to Job also comes from an ancient source.

The Old Testament passage traditionally taken to refer to Satan's rebellion is Isaiah 14:12-15:

> How you are fallen from heaven
> O Day Star, son of Dawn!
> How you are cut down to the ground,
> you who laid the nations low!
> You said in your heart,
> "I will ascend to heaven;
> above the stars of God I will set my throne on high;
> I will ascend above the heights of the clouds,

2

I will make myself like the Most High."
But you are brought down to Sheol, to the depths of the Pit.

In Genesis we read how Satan influenced our first parents to repeat his own rebellion. Russier says of this passage,

> The serpent is the agent, the spokesman of this power, a power superior to man's, more conscious in its intentions, more subtle in its activities. It knows the heart of man and knows how to reach it but its penetration is not the product of love. It is a jealous and evil power, and it is clearly God's enemy. . . . In veiled and enigmatic fashion the Yahwist uses the more than animal features in the figure of the serpent to suggest a power inimical to God which helps to bring about man's apostasy from God and which presents a deadly threat to the life of man in every age.[2]

The story of Adam and Eve portrays human evil as voluntary personal rebellion against the command of God. All three traditional sources of temptation—the world, the flesh and the devil—appeal to Adam and Eve. The devil reveals his deceitful character by telling Eve she will not die if she eats the fruit. He also manipulates the worldly desire for power: you will be like God, knowing good and evil; you won't have to obey. He also uses the flesh, the lure of the senses: the fruit is beautiful and looks good to eat.

In this episode, note how the devil takes good things and manipulates them to an evil purpose, the characteristic tactic of this apparent angel of light. The desire to know is good, so he turns it into a weapon of power: know that you may be like God. The desire to enjoy food is good, so he uses it to lure mankind beyond the limits God has set. The result of his action is separation and division from God—"I heard the sound of thee in the garden, and I was afraid, because I was naked; and I hid myself" (Gn. 3:10)—and estrangement from one another—"They sewed fig leaves together and made themselves aprons" (Gn. 3:7).

The story in Genesis does not end with mankind's rebellion. Rather, God comes looking for his creatures. He renders judgment not only on Adam and Eve but also on the serpent, who is thus clearly shown as subject to God (Gn. 3:8-19). Evil therefore is not as powerful as good, despite its tragic consequences.

The subjection of the devil to God is also graphically portrayed in the book of Job, where Satan must obtain God's permission before afflicting Job (Job 1:6-12, 2:1-6).

Another interesting passage is I Kings 22:19-23, where God seems to make use of a lying spirit to induce King Ahab into a disastrous war that will punish him for his crimes.

In Zechariah 3:1-4, Satan again serves God's purposes:

> Then he showed me Joshua the high priest standing before the angel of the Lord, and Satan standing at his right hand to accuse him. And the Lord said to Satan, "The Lord rebuke you, O Satan! The Lord who has chosen Jerusalem rebuke you! Is not this a brand plucked from the fire?" Now Joshua was standing before the angel, clothed with filthy garments. And the angel said to those who were standing before him, "Remove the filthy garments from him." And to him he said, "Behold, I have taken your iniquity away from you, and I will clothe you with rich apparel."

Here Satan is clearly the accuser, yet, as in Job, he seems to have a role among God's servants, perhaps representing the claims of God's justice in opposition to the divine mercy.

By the time of the writer of Wisdom, Satan is not only man's enemy but God's. "For God created man for incorruption, and made him in the image of his own eternity, but through the devil's envy death entered the world, and those who belong to his party experience it" (2:23-24). While the Old Testament does take over some elements of its demonology from other religions of the ancient Near East, it interprets them within the framework of the revelation of Yahweh. The reader must be careful not to mistake a similarity of names and symbols for an identity of concepts.

Old Testament Jewish thought differs from philosophical dualism in at least two ways. Not only are evil forces ultimately subject to God who is entirely good, but their influence on human beings does not abridge human freedom. In the story of Adam and Eve, human beings are portrayed not as hapless victims of a malicious evil power but as free agents choosing to join such a power in rebelling against their Creator.

Furthermore, the spiritual sources of evil are not meant to be appeased. Rather, all contact is forbidden. The Hebrew prophets repeatedly describe other religions as demon-controlled and insist that any dalliance with them is idolatry, a violation of the First Commandment.

Although the scriptural theology of evil differs from the approach of pagan religions, Scripture scholars may be tempted to dismiss it as equally primitive and unsophisticated. Is it not superstitious to attribute illnesses to spiritual beings and to seek healing in incantations and herbs?

Actually, the important question about the notion of a personal devil is not whether it is primitive but whether it is true. For the time being, we will bracket this question and continue to trace the historical development of the concept of evil and the demonic in Scripture, giving special attention to the teaching and ministry of Jesus Christ.

Auguste Valensin summarizes the role of Satan in the Old Testament as follows:

> In the Old Testament, indeed, Satan is of very little importance; his empire has not yet been revealed. It is in the New Testament that he is shown up as the chief of the coalition of evil forces—and when he is unmasked he is seen to be defeated.[3]

Jesus' attitude toward the realm of evil and evil spirits is crucial. If there are such beings intent on subverting God's order by enlisting all the forces of creation in its own undoing, these spiritual beings cannot be detected by physical observation alone. A positivistic, naturalistic science which limits itself to what it can observe and reproduce by the five senses can never prove the existence of purely spiritual beings, good or evil. The best it can do is posit them in order to explain physical phenomena for which it finds no better explanation (for example, restoration of life to one three days dead [Jn. 11:1-44]; instantaneous cure of widespread terminal cancer; the exhibition of gravity-defying events; or knowledge of events not humanly possible to know).

No, if we are to have evidence of spiritual realities, our best witness is a spiritual being who belongs to the world of spirits and also to the world of human beings. Such a witness exists in the incarnate Son of God, Jesus Christ, who not only encounters and deals with evil spirits but also performs miracles admitting no explanation by natural laws. How does Jesus of Nazareth treat the existence of evil spirits?

Jesus, the Son of God, enters the world in order to destroy the power of Satan and liberate human beings from his dominion (1 Jn.

3:8). Sensing this, Satan turns his fury against Jesus and his followers. At the very beginning of Jesus' public life, the Evil One tries to make him unfaithful to his mission.

The devil tempts Christ in the arid, pathless desert, the traditional abode of evil spirits. There Jesus overcomes the tempter in this first battle of the war pitting the Way, the Truth and the Life against confusion, deceit and death.

First Satan probes Jesus' relationship to himself, then to other people, finally to the devil himself. In each case he seeks to deflect Jesus from submitting totally to his Father's will.

The devil begins by taking advantage of Jesus' physical situation. "Use your power to help yourself, to meet your needs," he suggests. Jesus is hungry; his preparatory fast is over, and it would have been proper for him to eat. However, Jesus keeps his orientation to the will of his Father and rebukes Satan with a word from Scripture.

Catching on quickly, the devil begins the next temptation with a passage from Scripture. He will put on piety and show Jesus a quick and easy way in which the curious and sensation-hungry crowd can see and hear what it wants to see and hear and be brought to faith. This would satisfy the curious—or perhaps overwhelm them. Jesus, however, knows that the word of God is like a seed falling quietly into the ground without benefit of bulldozer or backhoe. People will neither be startled nor scared into the kingdom. They must come by repentance and change of heart.

In the third temptation, Satan reveals his true nature: he wants to be God. "Fall down and adore me; I will give you all the kingdoms of the world." Jesus knows that his kingdom is not of this world. "Begone, Satan," he commands.

Thus Jesus begins his ministry. After confronting the devil directly, he moves about Galilee preaching repentance and undoing the effects of Satan's work. Again and again his ministry is summarized in words like these: "And he went all through Galilee, preaching in their synagogues and casting out devils" (Mk. 1: 39). "It was just then that he cured many people of their diseases and afflictions and of evil spirits, and gave the gift of sight to many who were blind" (Lk. 7:21).

That the blind should see, the lame walk, and the deaf hear had been predicted of the Messiah, the compassionate servant who was to take on himself the iniquity of all humanity. The Messiah would lift the burden of sin and suffering and break the tyranny of Satan. He would bring a remedy for spiritual evils and for those physical evils that symbolize and result from spiritual evils.

Thus Jesus begins the process of weakening and destroying Satan's power. He commands the Evil One with a word. "That evening they brought to him many who were possessed with demons; and he cast out the spirits with a word, and healed all who were sick" (Mt. 8:16).

Jesus sees the Evil One at work not only in hatred, self-centeredness and falsehood, but in many bodily sicknesses. Here are some cases where healing is consequent upon driving out demons:

A dumb demoniac receives his speech (Mt. 9:32-33).

A blind and dumb possessed man is healed (Mt. 12:22).

A woman possessed by a spirit and bent over for 18 years straightens up (Lk. 13:10-13).

Do these examples indicate that Jesus viewed the sick and the possessed as identical? No, the Gospels and the book of Acts seem to make a clear distinction between healing and driving out devils:

> A great multitude of people . . . came to hear him and to be healed of their diseases; and those who were troubled with unclean spirits were cured (Lk. 6:17-18).

> In that hour he cured many of diseases and plagues and evil spirits, and on many that were blind he bestowed sight (Lk. 7:21).

> Heal the sick, raise the dead, cleanse lepers, cast out demons (Mt. 10:8).

> And he called the twelve together and gave them power and authority over all demons and to cure disease (Lk. 9:1).

> These signs will accompany those who believe: in my name they will cast out demons . . . they will lay their hands on the sick and they will recover (Mk. 16:17-18).

> For unclean spirits came out of many who were possessed, crying with a loud voice; and many who were paralyzed or lame were healed (Acts 8:7).

Jesus heals many individuals without driving out demons, for

7

example, Peter's mother-in-law who is feverish (Mk. 1:30-31), a leper (Mk. 1:40-45) and two blind men (Mt. 9:27-30).

In both kinds of case, disease or disease symptoms are present, yet sometimes Jesus casts out demons and sometimes he simply heals the illness. For example, in Mark 7:1-37 Jesus heals a man who is deaf and dumb, yet in Matthew 9:32-33 a dumb man brought to Jesus is healed by casting out a devil. Rather than attributing all illness to spiritual causes, Jesus seems to be able to distinguish one type from another. Furthermore, he is able to deal effectively with both. This gives strong credence to his diagnosis.

There is a growing recognition in the medical field that many physical impairments have a psychological origin; psychosomatic medicine is quite respectable. Is it conceivable that the next medical breakthrough will be the recognition that some ills have a spiritual origin? If so, the resulting holistic medicine might even be a holy medicine! Even in the realm of physical illnesses with physical causes, diagnosis is often only probable. Many things can cause an elevated temperature, and not all of them are readily detectable by laboratory tests.

On the other hand, our psychiatric wards are filled with diagnosed but unhealed patients. This may indicate that the causes of mental and emotional illnesses are difficult to determine on the basis of symptoms. It just might be possible that in some cases the cause is demonic activity. Apart from some spiritual illumination or discernment, one cannot definitely ascribe a material event which could have natural causes to spiritual causes. A high probability is the best that unaided reason can do.

Let us return to the treatment of exorcism and healing in the Gospels. "They carried to him all those afflicted with various diseases and racked with pain: the possessed, lunatics, the paralyzed. He cured them all" (Mt. 4:24).

This passage mentions categories of ills—physical illness, mental illness, demon possession. This clearly indicates that people of the time recognized a difference between mental illness and possession. They lived much closer to illness than we do: those who were ill stayed in the home until they died, as did those who were mentally or emotionally disturbed, unless these were violent. As a consequence, people were more familiar with various illnesses and their symptoms than we are. It is a bit naive to suggest that they

The Testimony of Scripture

could not distinguish physical illness, emotional illness and demonic activity.

Jesus, too, recognized distinct sources of human illness. He is not simply adopting his contemporaries' speech and thought patterns. In fact, Jesus takes care to be exact in his diagnoses; he is *less* inclined to attribute afflictions to an evil spirit than are his contemporaries.

Not only does Jesus heal without casting out demons, he also drives out demons whose effect has not been physical illness but some other disturbance:

> And in the synagogue there was a man who had the spirit of an unclean demon, and he cried out with a loud voice, "Ah! What have you to do with us, Jesus of Nazareth? Have you come to destroy us? I know who you are, the Holy One of God." But Jesus rebuked him, saying, "Be silent, and come out of him!" And when the demon had thrown him down in the midst, he came out of him, having done him no harm (Lk. 4:33-35).

> And demons also came out of many, crying, "You are the Son of God!" But he rebuked them, and would not allow them to speak, because they knew that he was the Christ (Lk. 4:41).

> And whenever the unclean spirits beheld him, they fell down before him and cried out, "You are the Son of God." And he strictly ordered them not to make him known (Mk. 3:11-12).

> But immediately a woman, whose little daughter was possessed by an unclean spirit, heard of him, and came and fell down at his feet. . . . And she begged him to cast the demon out of her daughter. . . . And he said to her, "For this saying you may go your way; the demon has left your daughter." And she went home, and found the child lying in bed, and the demon gone (Mk. 7:25-30).

Mark 9:14-30 recounts the episode of the boy afflicted with a dumb spirit. The symptoms seem to be those of epilepsy. Jesus does not lay his hand on the lad to heal him, as he usually does. He says, "You dumb and deaf spirit, I command you, come out of him, and never enter him again." Jesus instructs his disciples that in instances of this sort the approach must be that of faith and prayer. (That this kind of possession may take place without the cooperation of the person involved is clear from this episode, since the boy had been troubled from childhood, at a stage when informed consent could not have been given.)

Mark 5:2-20 is perhaps the most detailed account of Jesus' confrontation with an evil spirit, and it belongs to the oldest stratum of the Gospel. The man cannot be controlled but dwells among the tombs (an indication of his uncleanness) under the influence of the evil spirit. He is possessed of demonic power and strength. Anguished and violent, he has a spirit of self-destruction. Recognizing Jesus, the Holy One, he is tortured. Jesus demands the name of the spirits, then commands them to leave and go into a herd of pigs, which manifest that spirit of self-destruction by hurling themselves down the cliff into the sea where they are drowned, to the terror of the observers. The man is restored to normality by a word and desires to follow Jesus. The Gospel gives no indication that the man is ill. Modern practitioners might call him schizophrenic, but schizophrenia is not ordinarily healed by an exorcism.

Again, in his ministry Jesus sometimes simply heals the sick, sometimes simply casts out demons and sometimes heals those whose sickness has been caused by demons. He does not debate the existence or nature of devils but merely recognizes their reality and liberates people from their influence.

Jesus is relentless in exposing Satan's activity. He is not afraid to say to the religious leaders, "You belong to your father, the devil, and you want to carry out your father's desire" (Jn. 8:44). No wonder Satan fights back!

The devil, that "angel of light," here appears as the guardian of the Old Covenant. Scripture makes it very clear that the death of Jesus is a result of the plan and action of Satan: "The devil put it into the heart of Judas to betray him" (Jn. 13:2). "This is your hour and the power of darkness" (Lk. 22:53). Of course, Christians also know that the death of Jesus is an essential element in God's plan for the world's redemption and see in his resurrection God's vindication over Satan.

This perspective emerges clearly in the book of Revelation. Here the church's struggle against the forces of evil is portrayed in graphic terms and identified with Christ's battle against the devil and his angels.

In Revelation, demonic power is manifest in the great dragon, the beast and the false prophet (a caricature of the Trinity). The dragon is the caricature of the Father who confers upon the beast "his own power and his throne and his worldwide authority" (Rev. 13:2). In a parody of the resurrection, one head of the beast is healed after apparently receiving a death-blow (Rev. 13:3). Worshippers of the dragon and the beast chant hauntingly familiar phrases: "Who can compare with the Beast? How could anybody defeat him?" (Rev. 13:4). Only worshippers of the Lamb, knowing the final outcome, can appreciate the irony of these perverted praises.

The woman in Revelation 12 is the mother of the Messiah. By the birth of the Messiah, John means not the nativity but the crucifixion. Jesus, who was crucified under the inscription, "Jesus of Nazareth, King of the Jews" (Jn. 19:19), "was proclaimed Son of God in all his power through his resurrection" (Rom. 1:4). Thus the birthday of the king is the time of his enthronement. That is why the child is no sooner born than he is snatched away to God and to the throne.

Jesus' victory upon the cross has its counterpart in heaven, where Michael and his angels wage war upon the dragon and his angels. There is great rejoicing in heaven at the decisive defeat of Satan; however, the body of Christ must continue to struggle against the Enemy.

If the cross is the point at which Jesus enters upon his kingly glory, it is also the point where Mary enters into the fullness of her motherhood. She becomes the symbol of the Christian community, which brings forth Jesus in its members. As a symbol of the church, the woman is unceasingly attacked. "Then the dragon went away to wage war on the rest of her children" (Rev. 12:17). Hence this image of the struggle of the woman with the dragon portrays the actual situation of the church at any moment of time in the face of the demonic. Satan wages war on the church, and the church must resist and continue Christ's victory until Satan is finally crushed for all time.

11

2. THE TESTIMONY OF THE FATHERS

Having examined Scripture for evidence of how Jesus and the New Testament church dealt with evil spirits, we turn next to the witness of the church Fathers. How did the early church experience Satanic opposition, and how did it handle this? As might be expected, the Fathers discuss demonic activity in conjunction with pastoral practice. Their concern is not to argue for the devil's existence but to protect Christians from his unwanted incursions and to liberate from his kingdom those preparing for baptism.

The ministry of healing and deliverance is seen by the Fathers as a logical extension of Christ's ministry. Justin Martyr writes,

> For He also became man, as we stated, and was born in accordance with the will of God the Father for the benefit of believers, and for the defeat of demons. Even now, your own eyes will teach you the truth of this last statement. For many demoniacs throughout the entire world, and even in your own city, were exorcised by many of our Christians in the name of Jesus Christ, who was crucified under Pontius Pilate; and our men cured them, and they still cure others by rendering helpless and dispelling the demons who had taken possession of these men, even when they could not be cured by all the other exorcists, and the exploiters of incantations and drugs.[4]

Since demons are identified as the deities of pagan religions, it is no surprise that the preaching of the gospel to pagans provokes demonic opposition and is accompanied by signs such as deliverance and healing. The *Acts of Thomas*, generally ascribed to the end of the second century, regards the expulsion of evil spirits as the normal byproduct of preaching the gospel, and St. Irenaeus writes,

> Wherefore, also, those who are in truth his disciples, receiving grace from him, do in his name perform [miracles], so as to

promote the welfare of other men, according to the gift which each one has received from him. For some do certainly and truly drive out devils, so that those who have thus been cleansed from evil spirits frequently both believe [in Christ], and join themselves to the church.[5]

In fact, exorcism is often cited as proof of the power of Christianity and the falsehood of pagan religions. For example, Lactantius indicates that by the prayer of Christians devils are forced to reveal their names; he declares that the sign of the cross is particularly efficacious in repelling evil spirits:

At present it is sufficient to show what great efficacy the power of this sign has. How great a terror this sign is to the demons, he will know who shall see how, when adjured by Christ, they flee from the bodies which they have besieged. For as he himself, when he was living among men, put to flight all the demons by his word, and restored to their former senses the minds of men which had been excited and maddened by their dreadful attacks; so now his followers, in the name of their Master, and by the sign of his passion, banish the same polluted spirits from men. And it is not difficult to prove this. For when they sacrifice to their gods, if any one bearing a marked forehead stands by, the sacrifices are by no means favorable. "Nor can the diviner, when consulted, give answers." . . . for this must necessarily be the true religion, which both understands the nature of demons, and understands their subtlety, and compels them, vanquished and subdued, to yield to itself. . . . But, in truth, the same demons, when adjured by the name of the true God, immediately flee. What reason is there why they should fear Christ, but not fear Jupiter, unless that they whom the multitude esteem to be gods are also demons?[6]

Minucius Felix also identifies pagan gods as demons.

A great many, even some of your own people, know all those things that the demons themselves confess concerning themselves, as often as they are driven by us from bodies by the torments of our words and by the fires of our payers. Saturn himself, and Serapis, and Jupiter, and whatever demons you worship, overcome by pain, speak out when they are; and assuredly they do not lie to their own discredit, especially when any of you are standing by. Since they themselves are the witnesses that they are demons, believe them when they confess the truth of themselves; for when abjured by the only and true God, unwillingly the wretched beings shudder in their bodies, and either at once leap forth, or vanish by degrees, as the faith of the sufferer assists or the grace of the healer inspires. Thus they fly from Christians when near at hand, whom at a distance they harassed by your means in their assemblies. And thus, introduced into the minds of the ignorant, they secretly sow there a hatred of us by means of fear. For it is natural both to hate one whom you fear, and to injure one whom you have feared, if you can. Thus they take possession of the minds and obstruct the hearts, that men may begin to hate us before they know us; lest, if known, they should either imitate us, or not be able to condemn us.[7]

Later, St. Ambrose gives an account of the power of saints' relics against evil spirits; he uses this as an apologetic against heretics who deny the reality of evil spirits:

Why should I use many words? God favored us, for even the clergy were afraid who were bidden to clear away the earth from the spot before the chancel screen of SS. Felix and Nabor. I found the fitting signs, and on bringing in some on whom hands were to be laid, the power of the holy martyrs became so manifest, that even whilst I was still silent, one was seized and thrown prostrate at the holy burial-place.... The evil spirits say to the martyrs, "Ye are come to destroy us." The Arians say, "The torments of the devils are not real but fictitious and made-up tales." I have heard of many things being made up, but no one has ever been able to feign that he was an evil spirit. What is the meaning of the torment we see in those on whom hands are laid? What room is there here for fraud? What suspicion of pretense?[8]

The early church, then, dealt with evil spirits whenever the need arose, and the experience was not uncommon. Tertullian testifies:

All this might be officially brought under your notice, and by the very advocates.... The clerk of one of them who was liable to be thrown upon the ground by an evil spirit, was set free from this affliction; as was also the relative of another, and the little boy of a third.[9]

Occasionally demons also had to be driven out of particular locations and even animals:

For ourselves, so far are we from wishing to serve demons, that

15

by the use of prayers and other means which we learn from Scripture, we drive them out of the souls of men, out of places where they have established themselves, and even sometimes from the bodies of animals; for even these creatures often suffer from injuries inflicted upon them by demons.[10]

The early church not only responded to demons it encountered, it also took the initiative by praying against demonic influence as a regular part of the initiation of catechumens. By and large, in the first few centuries these were adults who had been immersed in a pagan civilization, given to the worship of false gods—whom the Fathers term "demons in disguise"—and domiciled in a world in which spells, incantations and magical practices often served as a cover for demonic activity. To become a catechumen was to choose a new Lord, which meant one had to be freed from bondage to the old one.

The exorcism of catechumens was not a one-time prayer but a practice employed repeatedly during the long process of preparation for baptism. As Edwin Hamilton Gifford says in his introduction to the works of Cyril of Jerusalem:

> One of the earliest ceremonies, after the registration of names, was exorcism, which seems to have been often repeated during the candidate's course of preparation. "Receive with earnestness the exorcisms: whether thou be breathed upon or exorcised, the act is to thee salvation."[11]

We find accordingly that Cyril enforces the duty of attending the exorcism on all the candidates alike, and from his use of the plural (exorcisms) we see that the ceremony was often repeated for each person. Thus in the *Clementine Homilies* Peter is represented as saying, "Whoever of you wish to be baptized, begin from tomorrow to fast, and each day have hands laid upon you,"[12] the imposition of hands being one of the ceremonies used in exorcism. From expressions in the Introductory Lecture, "When ye have come in before the hour of the exorcisms," and again, "when your exorcism has been done, until the others who are to be exorcised have come,"[13] it seems that before each catechizing the candidates were all exorcised, one by one, and that the earlier, after returning from their own exorcism, had to wait for those who came later. The catechizing was thus frequently delayed till late in the day, and

Cyril often complains of the shortness of the time left at his disposal.[14]

Those who are baptized continue to need exorcism. St. Cyprian warns:

> And, on the other hand, some of those who are baptized in health, if subsequently they begin to sin, are shaken by the return of the unclean spirit, so that it is manifest that the devil is driven out in baptism by the faith of the believer, and returns if the faith afterward shall fail.[15]

Those who fall into apostasy are not to be restored to the church without exorcism. Vincent of Thibaris says that heretics who are reconverted should again be exorcised by laying on of hands.

Besides praying with individuals to be freed from Satan's power, the early church engaged in collective spiritual warfare. A very early reference is found in the letter of St. Ignatius of Antioch to the Ephesians:

> Be zealous, therefore, to assemble more frequently to render thanks [or to celebrate the Eucharist; the Greek word can have either meaning] and praise to God. For, when you meet together frequently, the powers of Satan are destroyed and danger from him is dissolved in the harmony of your faith. There is nothing better than peace in which an end is put to the warfare of things in heaven and on earth.[16]

As the previous quotation from Cyprian shows, the Fathers attribute the influence of evil spirits not only to pagan religions but also to sin: original sin, personal sin and habitual sin.

St. Augustine assumes his hearers are familiar with prayers of exorcism in the baptismal rite for little children; he uses this practice as an argument for original sin:

> Every man is born with this penalty and guilt. That is the reason, just as you have seen today, just as you know, even little children are breathed upon and exorcised, so that the hostile power of the devil who deceived mankind in order to gain possession of men may be driven out of them. It is not, then, a creature of God that is breathed upon and exorcised in infants, but him under whose sway all are who are born with sin, for he is the prince of sinners.[17]

Augustine's *Letter to Sixtus* and *Contra Julianum* continue the same argument.

17

In our debate against those who try, even though refuted at every point, to present God as the avenger of uncommitted sins, we run the risk of being thought to imagine such things about them, whereas they are not to be supposed so stupid as either to believe or to try to make others believe them. If I had not heard them say these things, I should not have thought them worthy of rebuttal. Confronted by the authority of divine writings as well as by the rite of baptism handed down from antiquity and firmly adhered to in the church, in which it is plainly shown that infants are freed from the power of the Devil both by exorcism and by the renunciation pronounced for them by the sponsors who carry them, and not finding any way out of their dilemma, these heretics plunge headlong into fatuity because they will not change their opinion.[18]

Is this your only reason for believing no one can stir up hatred against you concerning the baptism of infants?—as though any of us says you deny infants must be baptized; yet in your remarkable wisdom you say such extraordinary things as: they are baptized in the sacrament of the Savior, but not saved; they are redeemed, but not delivered; they are bathed, but not washed; they are exorcised and exsufflated, but not freed from the power of the Devil. These are the marvels of your judgments; the undreamed mysteries of your new dogmas; these are the paradoxes of the Pelagian heretics, more wonderful than those of the Stoic philosophers. While you are thus declaiming, are you afraid to hear: "If they are saved, what was sick in them: If they are delivered, what held them in the bonds of slavery? If they are washed, what unclean thing lay hidden in them? If they are free, why were they under the power of the Devil when they were not guilty of any wickedness of their own—unless it is because they contracted original sin, which they deny?[19]

In contrasting the Holy Spirit with evil spirits, the *Shepherd of Hermas* links the devil with some of what later come to be called the capital sins (pride, avarice, etc.):

In the first place, the man who has the spirit from above is meek, calm, humble. He abstains from all wickedness and vain desires of this world, and considers that he is inferior to all men. He does not give answers to questions, either, nor does he speak by himself (neither does the Holy Spirit speak when a man wishes him to speak), but he speaks then when God wishes him to speak. When a man who has the divine spirit enters a gathering of just men who have faith in God's spirit, and an entreaty is addressed to God by such a gathering, at that moment the angel of the prophetic spirit, who is attached to this man, fills him and in the fullness of the Holy Spirit he speaks to the gathering in accordance with the Lord's wishes. In this manner, then, the spirit of the Deity will be made clear.

"This, then, is the power of the Lord's divine spirit. Now I shall tell you," he said, "about the earthly spirit, that is inane, powerless and truly foolish. In the first place, the man who thinks he has a spirit exalts himself and wishes to have the seat of honor. Immediately he is reckless, impudent, indulges in considerable luxury and in many other deceits. He also takes pay for his prophecy, and makes no prophecy unless he receives it. Can the divine spirit receive money for prophesying? It is impossible for the spirit of God to do this, whereas the spirit of this kind of prophet is earthly. Furthermore, it does not approach gatherings of just men at all, but avoids them. It clings to the men who are doubters and to the vain, making prophecies to them in a corner, deceiving them by talk in accordance with their lusts—all in empty fashion, for their answers are to the empty. . . . But, put no faith in the earthly, empty spirit, because there is no power in him. He comes from the Devil."[20]

Similarly, the *Testaments of the Twelve Patriarchs* indicates a connection between evil spirits and the vice of drunkenness:

The spirit of fornication hath wine as a minister to give pleasure to the mind. . . . For discretion needeth the man who drinketh wine, my children; and herein is discretion in drinking wine: that a man should drink so long as he preserveth modesty. But if he go beyond this limit the spirit of deceit attacketh his mind, and it maketh the drunkard to talk filthily, and to transgress and not to be ashamed. Observe, therefore, my children, moderation in wine; for there are in it four evil spirits—of lust, of hot desire, of profligacy, of filthy lucre.[21]

The Fathers say several things about how exorcisms were performed in the early church. In the Greek *Euchologion* quoted by Kleopas, exorcism is described in this way:

And the priest breathes upon his mouth, his forehead and his breast, saying, "Drive forth from him every evil and unclean spirit, hidden and lurking in his heart, the spirit of error, the spirit of wickedness, etc."[22]

As indicated in this quotation, prayers of exorcism were worded simply; their core was the command to the demons to leave in Jesus' name. Tertullian underscores the efficacy of the name of Jesus:

> All the authority and power we have over them is from naming the name of Christ, and recalling to their memory the woes with which God threatens them at the hands of Christ as Judge.... So at our touch and breathing, overwhelmed by the thought of those judgment-fires, they leave the bodies they have entered, at our command, unwilling and distressed, and before your very eyes put to an open shame.[23]

Justin has a similar exhortation, and Origen emphasizes the straightforward simplicity of such prayer in Jesus' name:

> For every demon, when exorcised in the name of this very Son of God—who is the First-born of every creature, who became man by the Virgin, who suffered, and was crucified under Pontius Pilate by your nation, who died, who rose from the dead, and ascended into heaven—is overcome and subdued. But though you exorcise any demon in the name of any of those who were amongst you—either kings, or righteous men, or prophets, or patriarchs—it will not be subject to you. But if any of you exorcise it in [the name of] the God of Abraham, and the God of Isaac, and the God of Jacob, it will perhaps be subject to you.[24]

> For it is not by incantations that Christians seem to prevail (over evil spirits), but by the name of Jesus, accompanied by the announcement of the narratives which relate to him; for the repetition of these has frequently been the means of driving demons out of men, especially when those who repeated them did so in a sound and genuinely believing spirit.

> Such power, indeed, does the name of Jesus possess over evil spirits, that there have been instances where it was effectual, when it was pronounced even by bad men, which Jesus himself taught (would be the case), when he said: "Many shall say to me in that day, in thy name we have cast out devils and done many wonderful works."[25]

The Fathers attribute a similar power to the sign of the cross, as the quote from Lactantius earlier in this chapter illustrates.

The *Acts of Thomas* and the *Clementine Homilies* mention the laying on of hands in conjunction with exorcism. Tertullian records that exorcism was accompanied by anointing with oil and also by breathing upon the unholy thing, that the breath of the Spirit might put to flight any evil spirit. There are many later references to this breathing as a means of exorcism. In fact, it was included in the Ritual for Baptism used prior to Vatican II.

For the Fathers, the ministry of exorcism grew naturally out of the Christian's relationship to the Lord who decisively defeated the power of Satan. Justin puts it simply:

> And now we, who believe on our Lord Jesus, who was crucified under Pontius Pilate, when we exorcise all demons and evil spirits, have them subjected to us.[26]

However, this authority which belonged to all the baptized was most often exercised charismatically in the early church. That is, God gave certain individuals the ability to recognize evil spirits and deal effectively with them. This gift was conferred neither by baptism alone nor by ordination; it might be exercised by a priest or a lay person, male or female. As Gifford writes:

> The power of casting out devils, promised by our Lord, and exercised by the Apostles, and by Philip the Deacon and Evangelist, was long regarded in the early church as a direct gift still bestowed by the Holy Ghost, apart from any human ordinances. Justin Martyr, Tertullian, Origen, all speak of exorcism as being practiced by laymen, even by soldiers, and women, by means of prayer and invocation of the name of Jesus.[27]

The word "charismatic" need not suggest something bizarre or unusual. A pseudo-Clementine epistle, for example, treats exorcism as a normal way of serving a troubled brother:

> This also, again, is suitable and right and comely for those who are brethren in Christ, that they should visit those who are harassed by evil spirits, and pray and pronounce adjurations over them, intelligently, offering such prayer as is acceptable before God. . . . Let them, therefore, with fasting and with prayer make their adjurations, and not with the elegant and well-arranged and fitly ordered words of learning, but as men who have received the gift of healing from God, confidently, to the glory of God.[28]

Gradually exorcists came to be formally recognized and designated as such by church authority, though the exorcists were not necessarily themselves ordained. (Some texts indicate that they were ordained, others—like the one below—that they were not. Local practice evidently varied considerably.)

> I the same [James, the son of Alpheus] make a constitution in regard to an exorcist. An exorcist is not ordained. For it is a trial of voluntary goodness, and of the grace of God through Christ by the inspiration of the Holy Spirit. For he who has received the gift of healing is declared by revelation from God, the grace which is in him being manifest to all. But if there be occasion for him, he must be ordained a bishop, or a presbyter, or a deacon.[29]

Bishop Cornelius of Rome refers to this order of exorcists twice in his letter to Bishop Fabian of Antioch.[30] Another reference to this group of exorcists is found in a third-century narrative.

> ... there arose among us on a sudden a certain woman, who in a state of ecstasy announced herself as a prophetess, and acted as if filled with the Holy Ghost. And she was so moved by the impetus of the principal demons, that for a long time she made anxious and deceived the brotherhood, accomplishing certain wonderful and portentous things, and promised she would cause the earth to be shaken. Not that the power of the demon was so great that he could prevail to shake the earth, or to disturb the elements; but that sometimes a wicked spirit, prescient, and perceiving that there will be an earthquake, pretends that he will do what he sees will happen. By these lies and boasting he had so subdued the minds of individuals, that they obeyed him and followed whithersoever he commanded and led. He would also make that woman walk in the keen winter with bare feet over frozen snow, and not to be troubled or hurt in any degree by that walking. Moreover, she would say that she was hurrying to Judea and to Jerusalem, feigning as if she had come thence. Here also she deceived one of the presbyters, a countryman, and another deacon, so that they had intercourse with that same woman, which was shortly afterwards detected.
>
> For on a sudden there appeared unto her one of the exorcists, a man approved and always of good conversation in respect of religious discipline; who, stimulated by the exhortation also of very many brethren who were themselves strong and praiseworthy in the faith, raised himself up against that wicked spirit to overcome it; where moreover, by its subtle fallacy, had predicted this a little while before, that a certain adverse and unbelieving tempter would come. Yet that exorcist, inspired by God's grace,

bravely resisted, and showed that that which was before thought holy was indeed a most wicked spirit.[31]

The formal recognition of those gifted to perform exorcisms arose from a double need. On the one hand, the faithful had to be protected from such abuses as superstitious practices (charms, incantations and the like) and simony (see Acts 8:18-24). On the other hand, since catechumens were to undergo repeated exorcisms, designating certain exorcists ensured that this ministry would be performed without scandal or harm.

The ordination of exorcists is mentioned in 341 A.D.:

> The Holy Synod decrees that persons in villages and districts, or those who are called *chorepiscopi*, even though they may have received ordination to the episcopate, shall regard their own limits and manage the churches subject to them, and be content with the care and administration of these; but they may ordain readers, subdeacons and exorcists, and shall be content with promoting these, but shall not presume to ordain either a presbyter or a deacon, without the consent of the bishop of the city to which he and his district are subject. And if he shall dare to transgress (these) decrees, he shall be deposed from the rank which he enjoys.[32]

The Synod of Laodicea (343-381) further specifies that no one may exorcise without being officially named to the office of exorcist: "They who have not been promoted [to that office] by the bishop, ought not to adjure, either in churches or in private houses."[33]

By the fifth century, the office of exorcist had evolved into one of the minor orders preliminary to Holy Orders. The *Statua Ecclesiae Antiquae* gives a rite for the ordination of exorcist in which there is no laying on of hands; the bishop simply gives the candidate the *Book of Exorcisms*. Healing of the sick is not mentioned in conjunction with power over evil spirits.

Thus, over the course of 500 years, an unpredictable charismatic gift evolved into an ordained ministry exercised under church jurisdiction.

The Fathers of the early church saw evil spirits at work in the world, in pagan religions and even in Christians. These writers portrayed a vibrant church whose members did not hesitate to confront evil spirits in the name of Jesus.

The *Roman Ritual* used prior to Vatican II is an excellent summary of the pastoral practice developed by the church Fathers. Prayers of exorcism may be found both in the baptismal ceremony—which includes the sign of the cross, anointing with the oil of catechumens and the *"exsufflatio,"* or breathing out—and in the rite of exorcism for those obsessed by demons.

First, let no one readily believe that a person is obsessed by the devil but let him recognize these signs by which the obsessed differ from those who suffer from melancholy or some other disease. Signs of demonic obsession are to speak in an unknown language or to understand one so speaking; to manifest things that are hidden or happening at a distance; to manifest a strength exceeding one's natural capacity, and things of this nature. The more of these things occurring, the greater the certainty.

In order to better understand the situation, let the exorcist, after one or two exorcisms, question the obsessed person about what he is experiencing in his spirit or in his body so that he may be aware what words disturb the evil spirit most, so that henceforth these may be emphasized and repeated.

Let the exorcist be mindful of the various wiles and deceptions the demons use to deceive the exorcist for they are accustomed often to answer falsely or make themselves known with difficulty so that the exorcist may be worn out and leave off, or that the person may not seem to be harassed by the demonic.

Sometimes after they have been manifest, they hide and leave the body free of any annoyance so that the person thinks he is completely delivered. However, the exorcist ought not to leave off until he has seen signs of deliverance.

Sometimes the demons will arrange whatever obstacles they can lest the possessed yield to exorcisms, or they try to persuade the possessed that this is a natural illness. Sometimes during an exorcism they will put the person to sleep, show him some sort of vision, hiding themselves, so that the person seems to have been set free.

Sometimes the demons manifest an evil deed that has been done and by whom and how its effects are to be annulled. Take care that because of this one has no recourse to magicians or "wise men" or any other than the ministers of the church. Do not become involved in superstition or any other illicit way of action.

Sometimes the devil leaves the person alone and permits the person to receive the Eucharist so that he may seem to have

24

departed. Finally, the arts and deceits of the devil to deceive men are countless, and the exorcist is to be cautious lest he be deceived by them.

And so, mindful that Our Lord said this kind of demon is not cast out but by prayer and fasting, let the exorcist and others take care to use these two means of imploring the divine assistance.

The exorcism should take place in the church, if possible, or in some respectable and religious place, apart from the crowd. For good reason, if the obsessed person is ill, the exorcism may take place in a private home.

The troubled person should be advised, if mentally and physically able, to pray, to fast, to confess his sins, and frequently to receive the Eucharist. During the exorcism, let the person be recollected, turn to the Lord, and with firm faith and in all humility ask to be made whole. Even when more sorely troubled, let him be patient and trust in the help of God.

Let the vexed person have a crucifix in his hands or before his eyes. Relics of the saints may be reverently applied to the head or breast of the person. Care should be taken so that the sacred objects may not be treated unworthily or damaged in any way by the demon. . . .

The exorcist should not engage in much conversation or questions that are curious and not pertinent, particularly with matters hidden or future. He should command the unclean spirit to be silent and to answer only when questioned. He is not to be believed if he pretends to be the spirit of some saint or of some deceased person, or a good angel. The necessary questions to be asked are, for example, the number and name of the besieging spirits, the time they entered in and why, and things of this kind. Let the exorcist restrain all that is inept, trivial, or mocking, and pay no attention to such. . . .

The exorcisms should be made and read as a command, with authority, great faith, humility and fervor. When he sees the spirit greatly tormented, then he should be more insistent and urgent. As often as he shall observe the person experiencing disturbance in some part of the body, or being poked, or some swelling appear, let him there make the sign of the cross and sprinkle with holy water, which should always be ready.

Let the exorcist observe what words most disturb the demons and repeat them often. When he comes to threats, these should be repeated again and again, always increasing the punishment. If he sees that he is getting somewhere, let the exorcist persevere for two, three, four hours, if he can, until victory is gained. . . .

Let the exorcist use the words of sacred Scripture rather than his own. Let him command the demon to reveal whether he is possessing the person because of some magic art, or evil symbols, or instruments. These should be found and buried. Moreover, the troubled person should open to the exorcist all his temptations.

When the person has been delivered, he should be warned to beware of sin lest occasions be given for the demon to return and the last state become worse than the first.[34]

Through the centuries, the church has continued to take a militant stance against Satan and the works of darkness. Although her dogmatic statements have been few, her teaching and pastoral practice have been consistent and unequivocal.

In Chapter 1 we quoted the statement of the Fourth Lateran Council against Albigensianism. This statement identifies the devil as a being whom God created good but who became evil through his own rebellion. Note that this profession of faith ("We firmly believe and profess without qualification") does not question the existence of demons but accepts this as part of the church's ongoing tradition.

In summing up St. Paul's teaching, the Council of Trent clearly recognizes the role of Satan in salvation history. "Sinful man is under the power of the devil and of death," says the council. In saving us, God "has rescued us from the power of darkness and transferred us into the kingdom of his beloved Son, in whom we have redemption and the remission of sins," while those who sin after baptism "have given themselves over . . . to the power of the devil." (Other magisterial statements are included in Appendix I.)

The Fathers recognize degrees of affliction by the devil, ranging from temptations to possession by evil spirits. Origen, for example, writes:

It is then clearly established, by many proofs, that while the soul of man exists in this body, it may admit different energies, i.e., operations, from a diversity of good and evil spirits. Now, of wicked spirits there is a twofold mode of operation: i.e., when they either take complete and entire possession of the mind, so as to allow their captives the power neither of understanding nor feeling; as, for instance, is the case with those commonly called possessed, whom we see to be deprived of reason, and insane (such as those were who are related in the Gospel to have been cured by the Savior): or when by their wicked suggestions they deprave a sentient and intelligent soul with thoughts of various kinds, persuading it to evil, of which Judas is an illustration, who was induced at the suggestion of the devil to commit the crime of treason, according to the declaration of Scripture, that "the devil had already put it into the heart of Judas Iscariot to betray him."[35]

Naturally, different remedies apply to different cases. The Christian experiencing temptation can simply renounce the work of the Evil One; for someone whose difficulty is prolonged, the prayer of others with gifts in this area may be sought.

Among the Fathers we do not find a distinction between two types of prayer against evil spirits; formal exorcism seems to be used for cases of possession as well as for cases of more ordinary temptation. Wherever the distinction is first made, manuals of moral theology since the time of Alphonsus Liguori recognize a difference, pointing out that the simple prayer of deliverance can be prayed by anyone.

The church has always taught that the devil exists and that the person who wants to make progress in his Christian life must deal with him as well as with the world and the flesh. Theologians who dismiss him as part of an outmoded worldview are departing from a long and solid tradition.

3. THE INFLUENCES OF SATAN

In this chapter, we will take a closer look at Satan and how he operates, contrasting his work with the power and purposes of God. We will examine how evil can affect the human person, distinguishing carefully among temptation, obsession and possession. Finally, we will begin to see how the work of the Evil One can be undone, discussing the need for discernment and the ministry of deliverance.

Many have trivialized Satan by depicting him as a cartoon figure with horns, pointed tail, a pitchfork and red pajamas. This imagery does not originate in Scripture, where the devil is portrayed as an intelligent spiritual being, cunning and powerful. Of course, a spiritual being can only be described through images, and Scripture is rife with images of evil, from the serpent of Genesis 3 to the dragon and the beast of Revelation. Such images can communicate effectively. In *The Trilogy of the Rings*, for example, J.R.R. Tolkien creates unforgettable images of evil. The fact that a writer employs imagery does not reduce the reality he is portraying to the level of the symbolic. If a speaker says, "It's raining cats and dogs" and a hearer finds the lawn devoid of quadrupeds, he is not justified in concluding that the weather is not stormy. Similarly, the writer of Revelation may truly portray Satan as a dragon without implying that the Christian engaging him in battle needs flame-proof armor.

Louis Monden argues persuasively for the existence of a personal devil:

Actually, contemporary thought is prone to understand all mention of the diabolical in a figurative sense, and to look upon the Demon as a personification of the powers of evil. This personification of whatever symbolizes evil, found in the Old and New Testament literature, seems to them to be a part of that mythological garb in which God's entire message comes to us. In this matter, as in others, the existentialist theology of our day seeks to extract the marrow of Christian preaching from every myth, to free that preaching from outmoded conceptual schemes, and to translate it into a more authentic religious expression.

However, if one reads the Scriptures with an open mind, not bound by preconceived notions, it is easy to see that one cannot eliminate the demon as a personal entity without changing the Christian message in its very essence. As far as the authors of the New Testament were concerned—even beyond that, in the thought of Christ himself—evil is, first of all, not some thing but some one.

The struggle against "the Evil One" is of a strikingly personal character, and it is exactly for this reason that the battle on behalf of the kingdom of God, like the battle which marks our own work-a-day lives, takes on an earnestness, an inexorable dramatic tension, which is the very touchstone of a true Christian life. The custom adopted by Christians, since the last century, of "de-mythologizing" Satan often, therefore, takes on the nature of a flight from the serious exactions of the Christian situation.[36]

What, then, lies behind the images depicting Satan? What kind of being is he, what are his purposes for mankind, and what means does he use to further these designs?

We have already stated that Satan is a very powerful spiritual being. He is not a static set of circumstances or a tempting situation into which one may fall. Rather, he is on an active campaign for evil and destruction. As Peter puts it, "Be sober, be watchful. Your adversary the devil prowls around like a roaring lion, seeking someone to devour" (1 Pt. 5:8).

The nature and colossal dimension of evil today may make one feel that the devil's power has been unleashed. This happens whenever Christianity grows weak. However, it is important to remember that Satan is a defeated enemy whose power has been broken by the Son of God.

The seventy returned with joy, saying, "Lord, even the demons are subject to us in your name!" And he said to them, "I saw Satan fall like lightning from heaven. Behold, I have given you authority to tread upon serpents and scorpions, and over all the power of the enemy; and nothing shall hurt you. Nevertheless do not rejoice in this, that the spirits are subject to you; but rejoice that your names are written in heaven" (Lk. 10:17-20).

Satan's purpose is to take God's place, and he tempts human beings to the same arrogance. Although he promises the good life, his desire is to control and ultimately to destroy individuals and to undo the progress of God's kingdom by sowing division in the body of Christ. Let us examine these purposes more closely.

Satan's desire to be God is in sharp contrast to the desire to glorify God. Michael, the leader of God's army, bears a name that means "Who is like God?" (See the account of warfare between Michael and Satan in Revelation 12:7-12.) Although Satan tempts mankind to an ambition like his own—"You will be like God" (Gn. 3:5)—he uses this lust for power to lure people into worshipping him. "And the devil took him up, and showed him all the kingdoms of the world in a moment of time and said to him, 'To you I will give all this authority and their glory; for it has been delivered to me, and I give it to whom I will. If you, then, will worship me, it shall all be yours'" (Lk. 4:5-7). Because he wants to be the object of praise, he hates the praise and worship of the Father, Son and Holy Spirit. The Christian who is humble enough to give up his desire for absolute control, placing himself in trusting submission to the Father, has already defeated Satan.

A contrast closely related to this one is brought out by the word "occult," which means "hidden." Satan promises his followers knowledge and control of what is hidden: the future, the hearts of men, the secret, mysterious forces in the universe. Followers of Jesus, on the other hand, walk in faith, which is "the assurance of things hoped for, the conviction of things not seen" (Heb. 11:1). Instead of demanding to understand and control, they trust in the wisdom and power of God. As Peter writes:

> Without having seen him you love him; though you do not now see him you believe in him and rejoice with unutterable and exalted joy. As the outcome of your faith you obtain the salvation of your souls (1 Pt. 1:8-9).

The Christian's power against Satan, therefore, is in proportion to his unwavering trust in God.

The work of God is to unify everything under the Lordship of Jesus Christ: "For he has made known to us in all wisdom and insight the mystery of his will, according to his purpose which he set forth in Christ as a plan for the fulness of time, to unite all things in him, things in heaven and things on earth" (Eph. 1:9-10; see also Col. 1:15-20). Christ's love unites human beings with their Creator (Jn. 14:18-23) and with one another (Jn. 17:11, 20-24). Satan opposes

31

this work by separating individuals from God and from one another.

His purpose for individuals is to separate them from God's love. This may be accomplished through inciting people to rebel against God and to thrust away his love, or through convincing them that God cannot possibly love and forgive them. The end result of active rebellion or passive despair is the same: the individual destroys himself by separating himself from God, the source of life (Ps. 104:29).

Satan is "the accuser of our brethren, who accuses them day and night before our God" (Rev. 12:10). The writer of Wisdom identifies Satan as the source of death:

> For God created man for incorruption,
> and made him in the image of his own eternity,
> but through the devil's envy death entered the world,
> and those who belong to his party experience it (Wis. 2:23-24).

"A murderer from the beginning" (Jn. 8:44), he is the source of persecution against Christians (Rev. 12:17), who nevertheless triumph through Jesus.

> There is therefore now no condemnation for those who are in Christ Jesus. For the law of the Spirit of life in Christ Jesus has set me free from the law of sin and death.... What then shall we say to this? If God is for us who is against us? He who did not spare his own Son but gave him up for us all, will he not also give us all things with him? Who shall bring any charge against God's elect? It is God who justifies; who is to condemn? Is it Christ Jesus, who died, yes, who was raised from the dead, who is at the right hand of God, who indeed intercedes for us? Who shall separate us from the love of Christ? Shall tribulation, or distress, or persecution, or famine, or nakedness, or peril, or sword? As it is written, "For thy sake we are being killed all the day long; we are regarded as sheep to be slaughtered." No, in all these things we are more than conquerors through him who loved us. For I am sure that neither death nor life, nor angels, nor principalities, nor things present, nor things to come, nor power, nor height, nor depth, nor anything else in all creation, will be able to separate us from the love of God in Christ Jesus our Lord (Rom. 8:1-2, 31-39).

As Jesus himself, the Good Shepherd, states the contrast, "The thief comes only to steal and kill and destroy; I came that they may

32

have life, and have it abundantly" (Jn. 10:10).

Satan's purposes are essentially negative: he cannot create anything but can only seek to warp and destroy what God has created. In attacking the church, God's work of unity and love, Satan's plan is to divide Christians from one another, sowing dissension and mistrust. The means Satan uses to destroy individuals and to destroy God's work of unity include lies, illness and physical disasters. Although his power is limited by God's omnipotence, he can manipulate physical things to evil purposes, as shown in the book of Job. There are places in this world so permeated with the presence of evil that they may be considered the domain of Satan. Tertullian gives one such example:

> Why may not those who go into the temptations of the show become accessible also to evil spirits? We have the case of the woman—the Lord himself is witness—who went to the theatre, and came back possessed. In the outcasting, accordingly, when the unclean creature was upbraided with having dared to attack a believer, he firmly replied, "and in truth I did it most righteously, for I found her in my domain."[37]

The fact that evil attaches itself to places and objects is the reason the Catholic Church exorcises such things as water and salt before consecrating them for sacramental use.

Satan's primary weapon, however, is not manipulation of physical things but distortion of the truth. Jesus says that the devil "has nothing to do with the truth, because there is no truth in him. When he lies, he speaks according to his own nature, for he is a liar and the father of lies" (Jn. 8:44). Again and again the devil is identified as a liar and deceiver (1 Kgs. 22:19-23, Rev. 12:9), one who loves darkness and hates the light of God's truth (Jn. 3:19-21, Jn. 13:27-30), from whose dark kingdom people are delivered into God's light (Acts 26:18, Col. 1:13). Satan distorts the message of the kingdom and tries to take away the word of God as soon as it is received in a person's heart (Mk. 4:15).

In all this, Satan is so subtle and devious that it is difficult to discern his activity. Acts 5:1-5 recounts how Satan influenced Ananias and Sapphira to lie, ruining their good deed through deception. A later witness to the deceptive work of Satan is Justin:

For we forewarn you to be on your guard, lest those demons whom we have been accusing should deceive you, and quite divert you from reading and understanding what we say. For they strive to hold you their slaves and servants; and sometimes by appearances in dreams, and sometimes by magical impositions, they subdue all who make no strong opposing effort for their own salvation.[38]

Let us turn from Satan's nature, his purposes and the means he employs to his effect on persons. This can range from a fleeting temptation to full possession. A diagram may help:

DAIMONIC (psychological)

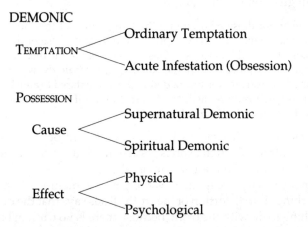

DEMONIC

TEMPTATION ⟨
  — Ordinary Temptation
  — Acute Infestation (Obsession)

POSSESSION

Cause ⟨
  — Supernatural Demonic
  — Spiritual Demonic

Effect ⟨
  — Physical
  — Psychological

The **psychological daimonic** is not in itself a work of Satan, although it may furnish the ground for Satanic activity. The daimonic is any natural function which has the power to take over the whole person, for example: sex and erotic love, anger and rage, jealousy and resentment, fear, craving for power. Every person, for example, has the urge to affirm himself, assert himself, defend himself, perpetuate and increase himself. In psychology this is sometimes called the primal energy, our most primitive instinct or impulse. Freud identified it with the libido or sex instinct, Adler with the will to power, Jung with the will to individuation. It is the source of initiative and creativity.

This source of power and energy can consume a person,

driving him to seek dominance in sports, art or business, or to be a perfectionist. Everything else is subordinated to this drive to be number one. However, success frequently causes such a person intense unhappiness.

Because the daimonic is so strong, it can easily be turned to an unworthy or an obviously evil purpose. A saint is consumed by the desire to give every ounce of his being for the glory of God; a sinner may turn the same zeal to exterminating people of a different race or persuasion; a man of unworthy ambition may be consumed by the desire to become a millionaire. The difference lies not in the intensity of the daimonic but in its end, and the fruit is not difficult to distinguish.

> While the daimonic cannot be said to be evil in itself, it confronts us with the troublesome dilemma of whether it is to be used with awareness, a sense of the responsibility and the significance of life, or blindly and rashly. . . . The way to get over daimonic possession is to possess it (take charge of it), take authority over it, by frankly confronting it, coming to terms with it, integrating it into the self-system . . . the patient is thus freed from morbid ties to the past.[39]

Because these basic drives are so natural, they often go unrecognized. However, failure to recognize the daimonic and come to terms with it may make people unwitting accomplices to destructiveness.

The psychological daimonic readily lends itself to manipulation by the demonic. However, C.S. Lewis points out in *The Screwtape Letters* that our immediate enemy is not so much the devils as the uncontrolled depths in ourselves. We need to be cautious about identifying as the devil that which may be the product of our unrecognized or uncontrolled psychological selves. The crucial question in distinguishing between the demonic and the daimonic is this: Is this condition the result of an external force acting on the person or a force within his own psychology?

In some cases, identifying the daimonic may help the person gain control over his problem. "Naked, essential evil can seldom be faced and dealt with other than imaginatively. . . . Seldom can one deal with anxiety or depression, with futility or isolation, until one turns these feelings into images. Doing this gives us something with which we can wrestle."[40] One may therefore speak of a spirit of anxiety or a spirit of depression or of loneliness, though what is really involved is instead the daimonic. Personifying the evil as a spirit may make it easier to handle. The danger of this tactic is that it may become a substitute for change rather than a means to change. Giving a name to a problem ordinarily makes the person feel better, but the diagnosis is not the cure.

What we have identified as the daimonic is related to what theologians have called the capital sins: pride, envy, anger, sloth, avarice, gluttony and lust. These are the roots from which specific sins spring. Nevertheless, the tendencies to evil in human nature are not in themselves evidence of the activity of evil spirits. Later I will discuss the capital sins in some detail, because Satan takes advantage of every tendency toward sin.

Ordinary temptations are thoughts and images the devil uses in attempting to turn Christians aside from doing God's will. He appeals to their desires and plays upon their weaknesses, the unruly inclinations of their natures. (See, for example, 1 Corinthians 7:5.) Satan's first appearance in Scripture is as the tempter (Gn. 3:1-6), and it should come as no surprise that the one who attempted to turn Jesus aside from the Father's plan for his life would seek to undermine God's work in his followers as well. The Wisdom writer warns:

> My son, if you come forward to serve the Lord,
> prepare yourself for temptation.
> Set your heart right and be steadfast
> and do not be hasty in time of calamity.
> Cleave to him and do not depart,
> that you may be honored at the end of your life.
> Accept whatever is brought upon you,
> and in changes that humble you be patient.
> For gold is tested in the fire,
> and acceptable men in the furnace of humiliation.
> Trust in him and he will help you;
> make your ways straight, and hope in him.
> (Wis. 2:1-6)

Temptations may also be **acute infestations** or **obsessions**. They are compulsive in terms of strength, persistence and continuity. They may play upon a moral, spiritual or physical weakness, or a combination of these, and the temptations of the devil are carefully orchestrated to produce maximum effect. While temptations are experienced as external to the person, in **possession** the devil acts from within.

> Demon possession is a condition in which one or more evil spirits or demons inhabit the body of a human being and can take complete control of their victim at will. By temporarily blotting out his consciousness, they can speak and act through him as their complete slave and tool. The inhabiting demon (or demons) comes and goes much like the proprietor of a house who may or may not be at home.
> When the demon is "at home," he may precipitate an attack. In these attacks the victim passes from his normal state, in which he acts like other people, to the abnormal state of possession. The condition of the afflicted person in the "possessed" state varies greatly. Sometimes it is marked by depression and deep melancholy, sometimes by a vacancy and stupidity that resemble idiocy. Sometimes the victim may be ecstatic or extremely malevolent and wildly ferocious. During the transition from the normal to the abnormal state, the victim is frequently thrown into a violent paroxysm, often falling to the ground unconscious, foaming at the mouth with symptoms similar to epilepsy or hysteria. The intervals beween attacks vary greatly from an hour or less to months. Between attacks, the subject may be healthy and appear normal in every way. The abnormal or demonized stages can last a few minutes or several days. Sometimes the attacks are mild, sometimes they are violent. If they are frequent and violent, the health of the subject suffers.[41]

In possession, the activity of the devil can be clearly distinguished from the personal activity of the individual and is, in fact, opposed to it. The evil spirit makes use of the person's body, speaking through his mouth and compelling his movements. The person's imagination and sentiments are often filled with the devil, sin and hell. He or she may be besieged by terrifying or impure visions, plunged into despair, convinced of damnation. While the devil directly affects sensation, imagination and feeling, his presence also influences intelligence and will, which become troubled, darkened, paralyzed, constrained.

I think I have encountered only three genuine cases of possession, along with two in which people were convinced they were possessed although they were not. The three cases which I regard as genuine were people who were deeply involved in sexual wrongdoing. One left before exorcism was completed. The other two required six to eight sessions before they were completely set free. Both of these were quite normal persons when the demonic was not in control. Both resisted actual exorcism, uttering threats of revenge, attempting to attack the exorcist and having forcibly to be restrained. During the prayer at times they became rigid, at times the face was distorted, assuming the appearance of an animal. On the other hand, the two who came because they felt they were possessed (but were not) described classic symptoms: both had a "spirit" within that talked to them, one had obscene visions and the urge to self-destruction. (See Appendix III for fuller descriptions of particular cases.)

We may distinguish two types of possession according to their origin: voluntary (**supernatural demonic**) or involuntary (**spiritual demonic**).

Supernatural demonic possession occurs when a person knowingly and willingly puts himself in a situation that invites demonic possession. The classic example is the story of Dr. Faustus, who sells his soul to the devil for the love of a woman. While this may seem to be the product of myth or medieval folklore, the situation it depicts is not uncommon: a person so desires a finite goal that to attain it he is willing to surrender anything, even eternal life itself. Such an attitude of heart may exist even in a person who would not acknowledge the existence of the devil or make an explicit pact with him.

Spiritual demonic possession takes place contrary to the person's will. There is no pact with the devil, either implicit or explicit. How can Satan gain control over an area of a person's life without an invitation on his part? Generally, this may occur when avenues of the conscious or subconscious mind are left unguarded. Thus, a child not yet aware of good and evil (see Mk. 9:14-29) may be so invaded, particularly if the environment is steeped in sin or subject to the occult. Invasion by evil forces may also occur when a person is unconscious either through accident, illness or anesthesia. It may take place when a habit of sin has left a person careless with respect to temptation and occasions of sin. Mental, moral or emotional weakness may also afford opportunity for demonic manipulation. Demonic forces may enter a person through emotional excess: hate, suspicion, terror and various forms of perverted sex. Attack is not inevitable in these situations, but it is possible and may be the cause of problems which are apparent only later. Possession may affect the person either physically or psychologically. In **physical possession**, the demonic power possesses the person's body and uses it as an instrument. This may cause the person to manifest extraordinary strength, climb walls, or move through the air—situations as bizarre to others as they are frightening to the victim.

In **psychological possession**, the demonic power uses the victim's psychological faculties. Thus the person may speak or understand a language totally unknown to him and reveal things which are hidden, such as the existence of buried treasure or others' secret sins.

Having considered how Satan can affect individuals, we turn to consider what can be done about it. Our concern at this point is not pastoral or pragmatic but theoretical, to understand discernment, deliverance and the various types of personal, group and official prayer.

The spiritual gift of discernment is extremely important. No formula can be given, for example, for distinguishing between demonic activity and disordered personality traits, between possession and mental illness, between obsession and possession. Yet these distinctions are crucial. To attempt to exorcise a person who is mentally ill may only exacerbate his conviction that he is incurably possessed.

Jesus gives the simple general rule for discernment:

> Beware of false prophets, who come to you in sheep's clothing but inwardly are ravenous wolves. You will know them by their fruits. Are grapes gathered from thorns, or figs from thistles? So, every sound tree bears good fruit, but the bad tree bears evil fruit. A sound tree cannot bear evil fruit, nor can a bad tree bear good fruit (Mt. 7:15-18).

However, the fruit is not easy to recognize, especially before it matures. St. Augustine expresses this well:

> There is, of course, no cause for wonder if even those possessed by a devil occasionally speak the truth about objects beyond the reach of their senses at the time. This, to be sure, happens by some

mysterious union with the evil spirit, so that the tormenter and his victim seem to be one and the same spirit. But when a good spirit seizes or ravishes the spirit of a man to direct it to an extraordinary vision, there can be no doubt that the images are signs or other things which it is useful to know, for this is a gift of God. The discernment of these experiences is certainly a most difficult task when the evil spirit acts in a seemingly peaceful manner, and, without tormenting the body, possesses a man's spirit and says what he is able, sometimes even speaking the truth and disclosing useful knowledge of the future. In this case, he transforms himself, according to Scripture, as if into an angel of light, in order that, once having gained his victim's confidence in matters that are manifestly good, he may then lure his victim into his snares. This spirit, so far as I know, cannot be recognized except by that gift mentioned by St. Paul, where he speaks of the different gifts of God: "...to another the distinguishing of spirits."

In other kinds of vision deception is not always harmful, but when the evil spirit has achieved his purpose and led someone to what is contrary to good morals or the rule of faith, it is no great achievement to discern his presence—for in that case there are many who discern for him. But the gift of discernment enables one in the very beginning (when the spirit appears as a good spirit to the majority) to judge immediately whether he is evil.[42]

In Chapter 5 we will further discuss the distinctions between possession and specific forms of mental illness. In general, it may be noted that, when the possessed person is not under attack, he is well-balanced and in control of his actions. He avoids all mention of the demonic as long as he is not approached on a spiritual level (e.g., in exorcism). During the attack, however, his personality is completely changed. He may take on a different voice, language, dialect, vocabulary, educational and cultural level. The demon refers to the victim in the third person, and the victim is ordinarily either unaware of what is going on or aware only as a spectator. The mentally ill person, on the other hand, speaks frequently and extravagantly about his supposed demon possession.

The most primitive exorcism is direct and concise, and the Lord himself gives it to believers in the Our Father: "Deliver us from evil." As many exegetes have pointed out, "Deliver us from the Evil One" is an equally valid translation. The *Roman Ritual* contains many such prayers, beseeching God for protection and help in times of temptation, spiritual danger, vulnerability and weakness. Many Christians have found it helpful to take refuge in Jesus under the aspect closest to their need, for example, in his purity, suffering or courage. The *Ritual* also contains commands to the evil spirit(s) in the name of God. This is from the ancient ritual for baptism: "Depart, you wicked spirit(s) and make way for the Holy Spirit," or, "In the name of Our Lord and Savior Jesus Christ I command you, spirit of [particular spirit may be named] to depart from our brother/sister and go before Jesus Christ to be disposed as he wills." The victim also may address the spirit in renouncing its work in his life, e.g., "I renounce you, spirit of condemnation."

Because exorcism is a command, it assumes the exorcist has authority to command. The account in Acts 19:13-16 is instructive. Impressed with the Apostles' ability to work miracles in the name of Jesus, some Jewish exorcists attempt to cast out demons in the same name.

> But the evil spirit answered them, "Jesus I know, and Paul I know; but who are you?" And the man in whom the evil spirit was leaped on them, mastered all of them, and overpowered them, so that they fled out of that house naked and wounded" (Acts 19:15-16).

A person who is not in right relationship to Jesus Christ cannot claim his authority over evil spirits. On the other hand, St. Paul urges all Christians to resist the Evil One both on their own behalf and on behalf of all Christ's men and women (Eph. 6:10-20; see also 1 Pt. 5:8-9). Because they are united in a single body (Eph. 4-6), all Christians have the power and the responsibility for protecting one another from harm, especially spiritual harm.

As a protection against abuse, the Roman Catholic Church has come to restrict the use of its official prayers of exorcism to those officially designated as exorcists. (See Appendix II.) There is an analogous situation regarding some of the sacraments. The risen Christ gave his followers the power to live in mutual forgiveness, but only an ordained representative of the community can extend the absolution that reconciles the penitent with the community. Any Christian can baptize in case of emergency, but a priest or deacon ordinarily celebrates this sacrament. Similarly, all Christians are to pray against evil in one another's lives and renounce it in their own, but only an authorized exorcist can pray the solemn exorcism to free a person from demon possession.

4. THE INFLUENCES OF THE CAPITAL SINS

In dealing with an enemy, the first requisite is to know him, to see whether one "is able with ten thousand to meet him who comes against him with twenty thousand" (Lk. 14:31). Like a wise general, the devil will not lay siege to the strongest part of the fortress but to the weakest. Therefore, a Christian seeking to free others from the work of evil spirits needs to understand the sources of moral, emotional and mental weakness. In the next two chapters we will consider the capital sins and many common mental and emotional illnesses. It would be absurd to conclude that all moral, mental or emotional defects are the devil's work; it is wise, though, to recognize that the devil can exploit and manipulate people through these avenues. If the minister of exorcism is not thoroughly conversant with the manifestations of the capital sins, he may either be ambushed or led astray in pursuit of the trivial instead of the essential.

From the earliest days of the church, spiritual writers have recognized a connection between root sins and besieging spirits. The *Shepherd of Hermas* says that the angel of wickedness

> ... is of a violent temper, bitter and silly.... When violent anger or bitterness comes over you, you can tell that he is within you. Then there arises the craving for excessive action, extravagance in many things to eat and drink, numerous feasts, varied unnecessary dishes, the desire for women, covetousness, arrogance, boasting, and a host of similar related excesses—when they arise in your heart you can tell that the angel of wickedness is within you.[43]

This description mentions anger, envy, gluttony, lust, avarice and pride, which will all later be included in the list of capital sins.

The adjective "capital" comes from the Latin word *"caput,"* meaning "head" or "source." These are the chief sins or sinful motivations from which many other sins come. The list of seven capital sins is the thoughtful product of human experience, an analysis that has endured through centuries. They are seven in number because seven is a symbolic number signifying fullness or completeness.

The distinction between sin and wrongdoing is an important one. Wrongdoing is an objective reality; sin implies that the person is accountable for what he has done wrong. Thus, for example, to drive on a newly paved street is wrongdoing, but it may not be sin if the street was not barricaded or posted, if a toddler released the emergency brake, or if someone disregarded the state of the pavement in order to rescue another person in grave danger.

The notion of objective wrongdoing, under constant attack in our society, implies a standard of right and wrong for human behavior. This means human beings are created with a God-given nature and a definite purpose. Just as a wrench cannot rightfully be used as a soup ladle, a person should not turn aside from his objective purpose: to know, love and serve God in this life and to be happy with him in the next, as the catechism puts it. Wrongdoing is to use a good thing for a base purpose, to "miss the mark" or "miss the path" (a literal translation of the biblical words for "sin"). The Bible assumes that there is a target and that one can distinguish between hitting the bull's eye and missing the target altogether.

No one possessing a ladle would deliberately try to dish up soup with a wrench. Why, then, do human beings deliberately engage in sin? To give a simple answer to a complex question, it is because human beings are not completely rational; they have drives, wounds and weaknesses that also influence their behavior. The great theologians call the human capacity for evil "original sin"; it seems to show itself spontaneously and early, even before the human person can reflectively choose to sin. The capital sins, also known as the seven deadly sins, specify or catalogue this innate tendency of human beings toward evil.

The distinction between wrongdoing and sin or culpability should warn the reader to avoid judging others. "We can recognize evil in others, but if we wish to look on the face of sin, we will see it most clearly in ourselves.[44] One can discern wrongdoing on the part of others, but only in oneself can one begin to discern sin, the responsibility for wrongdoing. Even in self-examination, scrupulosity on the one hand and callousness on the other can prompt serious misjudgment.

If love is the essence of human life, and if sin is missing one's purpose, all sin may be seen in terms of misdirected love. The capital sins of pride, envy and anger may be considered sins of absent or perverted love: the sinner seeks his own good at the expense of others. (It may be argued that this is not genuine self-love but only nearsighted selfishness.) Sloth is a sin of defective love; the slothful person loves nothing sufficiently to engage his energies. Avarice, gluttony and lust are sins of excessive love—of money, food and sex, respectively. The first three sins represent a fascination with personal superiority that excludes others. They are known as "cold sins." The last three involve a relationship with something or someone outside oneself and are known as "warm sins." Sloth, of course, is the "lukewarm sin."

Let us consider each capital sin in turn.

PRIDE

Webster defines pride as "inordinate self-esteem." St. Paul cautions, "I bid every one among you not to think of himself more highly than he ought to think, but to think with sober judgment, each according to the measure of faith which God has assigned him" (Rom. 12:3). The proud person idolizes and overvalues himself, attributing all his good qualities to his own merit rather than acknowledging the role of God's grace in his life.

The proud person exalts himself over others, often belittling them in an attempt to make himself look better. He disdains the give-and-take of community, preferring to ignore or manipulate others rather than serve or submit to them. He recognizes no standard of good and evil outside his own arbitrary choice. he "does his own thing," and when his "thing" is adultery, irresponsibility or apathy, his disregard for other persons becomes apparent.

Pride as a capital sin must not be confused with a healthy self-esteem. When one says, "Take pride in your work!" or "Have some pride in yourself!," one is using the word to mean "respect," both self-respect and respect for the integrity of one's work. Nor is it un-Christian to take care of oneself, to resist attacks on one's person, or to accept sincere compliments. Our Lord said, "Let your light so shine before men, that they may see your good works and give glory to your Father who is in heaven" (Mt. 5:16). The evil in pride is to glorify oneself rather than God, the source of all goodness, and to preserve oneself by seeking to destroy others.

Dante places the proud on the first cornice of Purgatory, thus showing pride as the first, the greatest, and in a certain sense the foundation of all the other sins. Because Dante sees sin as containing its own punishment, the way he depicts sinners in the *Purgatorio* paints a powerful image of the nature of each sin. Thus, the proud move slowly along bearing the weight of a great stone which so bows them down that they can see nothing but themselves. This is their punishment because in life they were so self-centered as to be blind to anyone or anything else.

Pride has this effect of blinding the proud individual. G.K. Chesterton observes:

> Looking down on things may be a delightful experience, only there is nothing from a mountain to a cabbage that is really seen when it is seen from a balloon. The philosopher of the ego sees everything, no doubt, from a high and rarefied heaven; only he sees everything foreshortened or deformed. Now shutting out things is all very well, but it has one simple corollary—that from everything that we shut out we are ourselves shut out. . . . Whatever virtue a triumphant egoism really leads to, no one can reasonably pretend that it leads to knowledge.[45]

The proud person cuts himself off from others and from God as well; it is pride, rather than finiteness, weakness or even sin, which separates individuals from God. The parable of the Pharisee and the publican (Lk. 18:9-14) makes this crystal clear, and St. Paul says, "I will all the more gladly boast of my weaknesses, that the power of Christ may rest upon me" (2 Cor. 12:9). St. Peter tells us that "God opposes the proud but gives grace to the humble" (2 Pt. 5:5).

Pride makes teamwork impossible, creating a football team with 11 quarterbacks and no coach. When each calls his own signals, there can be no unity of mind, heart or effort. Self-assertive pride determines "my good" with no regard for the common good; this breeds disintegration in the home, in the community and in society as a whole.

Pride has a great many daughters—or perhaps they should be called sons, for there is nothing feminine about these qualities. It is not difficult to see how this most fundamental of the capital sins gives rise to the others. Pride demands total control and thus feels threatened by the competence or prosperity of another (envy), by any affront or threat (anger). Sloth is too proud to let its complacency be disturbed. Avarice, gluttony and lust demand possession in order to guarantee dominance and security.

Pride's prolific progeny include boasting, hypocrisy, disobedience, competitiveness, stubbornness, discord and argumentativeness.

Boasting vaunts one's own excellence or achievement. There is a certain boasting which is relatively harmless because it is other-directed, a delight in something other than oneself. Thus, one can boast of one's country out of national pride and one's football team out of local enthusiasm. The fisherman can even boast of his catch, emphasizing the size of the fish rather than his skill as a fisherman: the sharing of such fish tales can be a form of convivial conversation. However, the boasting that reflects glory on oneself not only spoils conversation but soon becomes obnoxious. It often leads to exaggeration or prevarication.

Prevarication is the key element in hypocrisy, a word which means "to wear a mask" in order to make oneself appear more worthy of esteem. Isaiah reproached the professional holy people of his day, "This people draw near with their mouth and honor me with their lips, while their hearts are far from me, and their fear of me is a commandment of men learned by rote" (Is. 29:13), and Jesus severely castigated the Pharisees for their hypocrisy. In a civilization which honored holy men, they vaunted the trappings of religion while remaining far from its essence.

Because holiness and morality earn so little esteem in our society, hypocrisy may boast of sins or immorality. People want to appear worse than they are. College students, for example, may boast of fabricated orgies involving sex, drugs or alcohol in order to gain the esteem attached to certain kinds of evildoing.

Much hypocrisy is not so blatant. People attempt to impress others by wasting money as if they had a great deal of it, or by pretending to an intimacy with the well-known when at most they have but a nodding acquaintance.

Pride is the cause of disobedience, just as the temptation "You will be like God" caused the first act of disobedience. Superior to everyone, the proud person "knows it all." He accepts no advice and can submit to no one.

Because a proud person can yield first place to no one, he is highly competitive. There is a healthy kind of competition which challenges a person to use his talents to the fullest, but the competitiveness born of pride insists on proving itself superior to everyone else, even if the victory is achieved by cheating.

Stubbornness is another frequent companion of pride. The stubborn person clings to his position in the face of all evidence to the contrary. This can easily sow discord and argumentativeness. "Discord" means "a division of heart," not simply a difference of opinion but the inability to respect or tolerate a different opinion. The proud person has become so wedded to his notion that he regards any disagreement as an attack on his person and value. He will argue the most trivial contested point with virulence.

Because love is Jesus' first commandment, pride provides the handle by which Satan can most readily manipulate an individual, turning him aside from pleasing God in self-forgetful love.

The opposite of pride is humble love, going out to God and others instead of focusing on oneself. Humility must not be confused with a poor self-image. The word "humility" has the same root as the word "human": "humus," meaning "ground, dirt or dust." Adam was formed from the dust of the earth, and humility is the virtue which enables his children to keep both feet on the ground. Because it is such a human virtue, Christians must learn it from Jesus, "who, though he was in the form of God, did not count equality with God a thing to be grasped, but emptied himself, taking the form of a servant, being born in the likeness of men. And being found in human form he humbled himself and became obedient unto death, even death on a cross" (Ph. 2:6-8). His own invitation is, "Learn from me, for I am gentle and lowly in heart" (Mt. 11:29).

The humble person sees God at work in his life and acknowledges his total dependence on God. "By the grace of God I am what I am, and his grace toward me was not in vain" (1 Cor. 15:10). The humble person knows he is not a fully integrated human being and cannot become one by his own efforts. Rather, he trusts himself to God, "who began a good work in you [and] will bring it to completion at the day of Jesus Christ" (Ph. 1:6).

Envy

Envy is the love of one's own good perverted to the wish that other persons be deprived of theirs. The envious person is sad when another is benefitted or has anything good. He somehow believes that any good which comes to another lessens his own supply. If someone else is honored, he feels debased; if another prospers, he feels impoverished. The envious person cannot enjoy what he is or has, so dejected is he at what others are or have. He is always looking through the wrong end of the telescope, reducing the great to the small. Envy reduces ambition to meanness and pettiness, sabotaging healthy competition. Far from challenging a person to do his best, it makes him desire to see others do their worst. It is a sterile thing; like a slug, it spreads slime on what it cannot devour.

It is not envy to admire another and wish to emulate him, or even to regret that one is not as gifted as another. It only becomes envy when one sees the other's ability as a threat and a disgrace and begins desiring that the other lose his reward.

Nor is it envy to be sad when an unworthy person is elected or an incompetent person is promoted. Rather, these can be examples of a righteous response to injustice. Envy is bitter when a worthy person is promoted or elected, and it may label him unworthy in order to justify itself.

Dante describes the envious in Purgatory as having their eyes stitched shut by wire threads so that they cannot see the sun. While they lived, they could not bear to look upon joy, especially the joy of others which might have shone on them. Now they can see nothing at which to rejoice.

Envy spawns related sins. These include suspicion and discord, detraction and slander, dejection and regret.

Like pride, envy sows discord. However, this discord is not born of aggressive self-assertiveness. Rather, it "can smile and smile and be a villain." It sows the seeds of suspicion among friends, undermines reputations through sly innuendo, insinuates wrong motives for right actions. "That good marriage is quite obviously subject to strains and tensions that are hidden from us. . . ." "If you only knew the real man. . . . " The envious person speaks in suspended sentences, leaving the listener to suspect the worst.

The envious are filled from day to day with bitter regret for what they cannot be or have. Dejection is their characteristic emotional state.

Few people are untouched by envy, and few wish to face it; no one wants to acknowledge such mean-spirited vice. Because envy operates so subtly and spontaneously, the person who fails to recognize it is likely to be controlled by it.

Often envy lurks behind a charitable response. A person who fails to win a basket of groceries says, "I hope those groceries went to a person who needs or deserves them," but his actual conviction is that no one could be more deserving than himself. Envious impulses come unbidden, but one can then entertain them as a source of secret satisfaction: "At last someone gave her what she deserved." This satisfaction demonstrates the power of envy, even in the life of a Christian.

Envy is a sin against that charity which sincerely desires the other's good. Its antidotes are contentment with one's own lot and admiration of one's neighbor, the ability to rejoice when good comes to another.

The Christian seeking to root out envy must cultivate contentment and gratitude to God for the goodness in himself and the goodness he receives as a gift. Realistic expectations help foster such contentment: a person who does not excel in every area is not thereby a failure. God expects faithfulness and diligence; he does not castigate the servant for starting with fewer talents but he is angry when the servant fails to use the talent he has to further his Master's kingdom (Mt. 25:14-30). Christians must also remember that the Lord guarantees only treasure in heaven; on earth their greatest honor is to share the reproach which came to him (Jn. 15:18-21). The saints provide many examples of this godly contentment in which there is great gain (1 Tim. 6:6). As St. Paul puts it:

> Not that I complain of want; for I have learned, in whatever state I am, to be content. I know how to be abased, and I know how to abound; in any and all circumstances I have learned the secret of facing plenty and hunger, abundance and want. I can do all things in him who strengthens me (Ph. 4:11-13).

Besides contentment with his own lot, the Christian seeking to overcome envy would do well to admire and honor others for their achievements and to rejoice actively in their good fortune: "Outdo one another in showing honor.... Rejoice with those who rejoice, weep with those who weep" (Rom. 12:10,15). The description of love in 1 Corinthians 13:4-7 will do away with envy:

> Love is patient and kind; love is not jealous or boastful; it is not

arrogant or rude. Love does not insist on its own way; it is not irritable or resentful; it does not rejoice at wrong, but rejoices in the right. Love bears all things, believes all things, hopes all things, endures all things.

ANGER

Anger arises when a person's sense of justice or dignity is offended; a real, imagined or threatened attack on one's person or rights provokes anger which then seeks to repay, destroy or get even with the person perceived as responsible for the attack.

A common example of anger is a toddler's tantrum: when the child encounters a limit or obstacle, he feels threatened or put down. He reacts by howling and screaming, often lashing out physically and verbally at the authority figure who has blocked his will. Unfortunately, many outbursts of anger on the part of adults resemble such tantrums.

Thus the trigger for anger is contempt, whether that contempt is expressed or implied by its perpetrator or imagined by its supposed victim. Many people respond angrily to the imposition of limits or commands. They perceive this as an insult to their ability to manage their own affairs or order their own tasks.

Rightly proportioned anger in response to actual injustice is not a sin. Anger becomes disordered because of its intensity, its object or its cause.

Disproportionate anger overreacts to a trivial or unintentional slight. This is the person who reacts violently when someone passes him without a greeting or brushes against him in a crowded place.

Displacement occurs when a person takes out his anger on an object which has not injured him. The proverbial example is the harried executive who restrains his anger during work hours but releases it by kicking the dog or chewing out his wife and children when he gets home.

Anger for the wrong cause responds to a perceived hurt which is not unjust. Thus, a player whose team loses a game may slash the referee's tires.

Anger, envy and hatred may be difficult to distinguish. All three desire evil for another person. Envy responds to the other's success as a threat to its own exaltation. Anger responds to

51

contempt inflicted upon itself and seeks to even up the score. Hatred needs no provocation but simply seeks to destroy the other. So far we have been talking about instances when anger flares up as an emotion. These may indicate the presence of the capital sin of anger, but anger as an emotion is different from anger as a habitual stance. Not every angry outburst springs from the capital sin of anger.

It may be helpful to think of the capital sin as cold or smoldering anger in contrast to the hot anger which so often flares up in human interactions. Anger may begin with a specific occasion, but if it is harbored and nourished over a period of time it produces the capital sin of anger. This may be closer to what we call malice, or ill-will.

The vice of anger may be nurtured internally in at least two different ways. One person may continue to feed his anger by mulling over and embellishing the offense, plotting and anticipating revenge. Plans for revenge can take entire possession of such a person. His anger grows in ferocity until it breaks out in an orgy of aggressive violence. Another person may be afraid to express anger directly; he turns the anger against himself in guilt and depression, and the anger burns smokily, darkening his self-image and his relationships with others. Like a fire, this kind of anger may not be detected for a long time. It makes its victim very vulnerable to manipulation by evil powers.

Dante has those who are being punished for anger enveloped in a thick and acrid smoke:

Never wrapped a veil about my head
So gross in grain and gritty to the touch
As was that smoke which held us blanketed.[46]

The smoke has made the angry blind, and so they must guide themselves by hearing instead of sight. The flames of anger do not burn clear and bright, but rather with a thick and evil pall that obscures every consideration except revenge.

Many people are perpetually angry; if there is no cause for anger they will invent one. Usually these are people who have been physically and/or emotionally ill-treated in their childhood. Often they are not aware of why they are angry, but their subconscious harbors many hurts against which they are reacting. Physical, moral and emotional child-abuse is widespread in our society, and its emotional scars may trigger a great deal of violence, from teenage gangs to the violence of terrorism. Anger expresses itself in verbal and physical abuse. Many a mother, exasperated beyond endurance, will vent her anger by screaming at her children. Men frequently explode in anger when they encounter such work-related difficulties as a stubborn motor. Anger often vents itself in abusive words, words that leap out like flaming swords that cut and sear and burn. Thus the person who feels put down cuts others to pieces with his words. This sort of treatment almost invariably leads to quarrels, if not blows.

Besides abuse, bickering and strife, anger's unlovely offspring include curses, ill humor, impatience and destructive criticism. Anger produces pouting, resentment, rebellion and lack of forgiveness. It manipulates others into compliance by the threat of its displeasure; they may give in to an unreasonable demand in order to avoid creating a scene.

We have already mentioned depression and guilt as the fruit of anger turned against oneself. Someone hurts a person, but the offender is too powerful to confront. Instead, the victim begins to think, I must deserve such treatment. There must be something wrong with me. Such negative feelings about oneself can be very difficult to correct.

Sometimes, on the other hand, genuine guilt is avoided through anger. Instead of taking responsibility for his own wrongdoing, a person blames someone else and becomes very angry with that other person.

The remedy for anger is forgiveness from the heart. Wielding the weapon of forgiveness, one need not deny the reality of the hurt but can bind up the wound by loving the offender and desiring his conversion. To forgive wrongs requires a humility few possess. It is fostered by the experience of being forgiven by a gracious God who has every reason to take offense at the sins of human beings but rather goes on the offensive in extending mercy to them. (See the parable of the unforgiving servant, Matthew 18:23-35.) As Jesus instructed,

> Pray then like this . . . , "And forgive us our debts, as we also have forgiven our debtors; and lead us not into temptation, but deliver us from evil." For if you forgive men their trespasses, your

heavenly Father also will forgive you; but if you do not forgive men their trespasses, neither will your Father forgive your trespasses (Mt. 6:9, 12-15).

St. Paul further specifies this instruction:

> Bless those who persecute you; bless and do not curse them. . . . Live in harmony with one another; do not be haughty, but associate with the lowly; never be conceited. Repay no one evil for evil, but take thought for what is noble in the sight of all. If possible, so far as it depends upon you, live peaceably with all. Beloved, never avenge yourselves, but leave it to the wrath of God; for it is written, "Vengeance is mine, I will repay, says the Lord." No, "if your enemy is hungry, feed him; if he is thirsty, give him drink; for by so doing you will heap burning coals upon his head." Do not be overcome by evil, but overcome evil with good (Rom. 12:14, 16-21).

SLOTH

The English word "sloth" fails to carry the proper connotation. "Sloth" sounds like "slow," which suggests deliberateness, control, proper pace. However, the sin of sloth may be expressed in frenzied activity as well as idleness.

To understand the capital sin of sloth, we must turn to the word *"acedia,"* from the Greek word meaning "to have no care for." Thomas Aquinas says sloth is a kind of sadness which depresses the spirit to such an extent that it shuns activity as wearisome and boring. Sloth is not so much a state of inactivity as a state of being bored with or opposed to all activity. Action pursues a good, either real or apparent. Success, ambition, fortune, heroism, courage— these are all purposes or motivations capable of dispelling sloth. Unlike these, sloth lacks any goal and thus lacks that love which is the active pursuit of the good.

When a person fails to set priorities and goals but throws himself into the first task of interest that comes to hand, he may be frantically busy, but he fails to accomplish the most important task for this moment. Sloth came in not during the activity but earlier, when he refused to take responsibility for ordering that activity to the highest good.

The person who only does what is pleasant, appealing or easy accomplishes little. Would the pleasure of chiseling marble have sustained Michelangelo through years of hard work? He saw the glorious figure of Moses or the poignant grief of a sorrowing mother in the marble, and to disclose that beauty was such a value that even as an old man he outdid many younger men in his industriousness. Such vision alone can overcome sloth. As St. John of the Cross points out:

> Also regarding spiritual sloth, these beginners usually become weary in the more spiritual exercises and flee from them, since these exercises are contrary to sensory satisfaction. Since they are so used to finding delight in spiritual practices, they become bored when they do not find it. . . . Since they expect to go about in spiritual matters according to the whims and satisfactions of their own will, to enter by the narrow way of life, about which Christ speaks, is saddening and repugnant to them.[47]

Sloth must not be confused with weariness, for weariness occurs when one is exhausted from effort. Sloth will never make the effort.

Nor should sloth be equated with leisure or the lack of "useful" activity. Such "useless" activities as writing a sonnet, listening to a symphony, painting a portrait, playing the piano or contemplating a sunset are not slothful. Rather, something done for the simple joy of doing it can be the noblest form of activity.

Modern slang has many expressions for sloth. These include "hang loose," "play it cool" and "laid back." Dorothy Sayers describes sloth as "the sin that believes in nothing, cares for nothing, seeks to know nothing, interferes with nothing, enjoys nothing, hates nothing, finds purpose in nothing, lives for nothing and remains alive because there is nothing for which it will die."[48]

Dorothy Sayers also identifies several manifestations of sloth:

> The sin which in English is called sloth is insidious, and assumes such protean shapes that it is rather difficult to define. It is not merely idleness of mind and laziness of body. It is that whole poisoning of the will which, beginning with indifference and an attitude of "I couldn't care less," extends to the deliberate refusal of joy and culminates in morbid introspection and despair. One form of it which appeals very strongly to some modern minds is that acquiescence in evil and error which readily disguises itself as tolerance, another is that refusal to be moved by the contemplation of the good and the beautiful which is known as disillusion-

ment, and sometimes as knowledge of the world. Yet another is that withdrawal into an ivory tower of isolation which is the peculiar temptation of the artist and the contemplative, and is popularly called escapism.[49]

Sloth has many manifestations:

1) Procrastination—Unlike the Good Samaritan, the slothful person is reluctant to engage in anything which may prove costly. Rather, he puts things off beyond the proper time. As a consequence, one responsibility treads upon the heels of another. Feeling pressured, he rushes through tasks in order to get them done, without concern for doing them well or pleasing God in doing them. Some slothful people seem always on the verge of beginning something they never quite begin. This gives the false illusion of being busy although they accomplish nothing.

2) Weak-spiritedness—The slothful person gives up when the way to his goal becomes too arduous. This person wants to fly without going through pilot training and will not admit that genius is 90% perspiration, only 10% inspiration. He often says "I'll try" instead of "I will"; this means he wishes he could, but he will give up if too much effort is required.

3) Causeless irritation—Because he feels incapable of exerting himself, the slothful person becomes angry at anything that demands effort. He responds to a difficult task not by rising to the challenge but by feeling dispirited and put-upon. He is frequently irritated by the active and joyful person, and rancor develops. He lacks the energy to hate his rival; his response is one of lethargic indignation.

4) Useless activity, what Dorothy Sayers calls "whiffling activity"—This includes frittering away time in such activities as trashy reading, constant travel or curiosity about trivia. This is not the sustained curiosity that provokes invention and discovery. Rather, it is a means of passing time, which for sloth always hangs heavy. Another example of useless activity is daydreaming of the Walter Mitty variety. Building castles in the air to compensate for failure is the opposite of the creative imagination which spurs initiative toward success.

5) Wasting time—"Not to waste time" does not necessitate proceeding under a full head of steam all the time; the full head of steam need not indicate time well spent. However, time is the one

thing a person can never regain; once gone, it never returns. The habit of wasting time can be extremely difficult to break. A person who claims to have no time to pray frequently wastes a great deal of time during the day. In fact, a spirit of prayer—habitually living in the presence of God—is the best insurance against wasting time.

6) Trivial conversation—Herbs and perfumes lose their fragrance unless they are kept tightly stoppered; useless conversation is like unsealing the bottle. Some people keep talking long after they have exhausted their thoughts. Loquacity may relieve the speaker, but it burdens the hearer. The slothful person flits from conversational flower to flower without ever speaking seriously, profoundly or passionately about anything. He verifies the proverb: "The steam that blows the whistle never turns the wheel."

7) Inability to recreate—Recreation is intended to re-create, to renew or refresh. Shakespeare says, "Sleep knits up the ravelled sleeve of care," and good recreation is as important to the spiritual life as sleep to the physical life. One's spirit cannot always be on the stretch; the bow must be unstrung sometimes. A common mistake is trying to work and recreate at the same time: writing letters while listening to a symphony or reading while traveling on a bus. Although this may be a profitable use of time, it is not recreation. True recreation must absorb a person so completely that he forgets work, care and responsibility.

8) Sadness, low spirits—On the spiritual level, the slothful person is prone to feel sorry for himself. He has been living an exemplary Christian life and no one seems to notice. He has been curbing his sensual appetites and avoiding venial sin, and it is boring. So he lets down a little bit and then becomes depressed at his lack of self-improvement. This person substitutes self-improvement for pleasing God. Always falling short of his own expectations, he is sad. He no longer sees the goal as attainable, and so he surrenders to depression or despair. That courage needed for spiritual growth oozes out of him and he gives up the struggle.

Jesus is impatient with the sloth that renders people fruitless. He tells one parable of a tree that failed to produce fruit (Lk. 13:6-9) and acts out another by cursing such a tree (Mk. 11:12-14, 20).

The gift of the Holy Spirit opposed to sloth is fortitude, the ability to persevere in pursuit of a goal. No man can find the purpose of his life by looking at himself, in sloth valuing his ease above God's will and the good of others. Man's true purpose is found only in Jesus, who said, "I am the way, and the truth, and the life" (Jn. 14:6).

Someone has expressed the purpose of the gospel as "comforting the afflicted and afflicting the comfortable." In Jesus' invitation—"If any man would come after me, let him deny himself and take up his cross and follow me" (Mt. 16:24)—is found a threefold remedy for sloth:

Deny—Overcome self-concern;
Take up the cross—Overcome self-indulgence;
Follow—Overcome inactivity.

AVARICE

From defective love (sloth) we turn to consider excessive or disordered love.

Avarice or covetousness is the excessive love of money and the material goods it can buy. By extension, it may also apply to such external goods as pleasure, honor and power.

The miser in the strict sense does not use his wealth for pleasure or power; he is satisfied just to possess. One frequently reads newspaper accounts of recluses living in miserable apartments, cat food their sustenance. Only upon their lonely deaths does it become evident that small fortunes were hidden in those apartments without doing their owners any apparent good.

The passion for collecting and hoarding is not limited to money. Some, with as much taste as money, have amassed collections of great art that few were privileged to see, only to have the art dispersed upon their death by unappreciative or impoverished heirs. Others have collected beer cans or comic books with the same spirit of selfish acquisitiveness.

St. John of the Cross observes that there is also a spiritual form of avarice:

> Many of these beginners have also at times great spiritual avarice. They will be found to be discontented with the spirituality which God gives them. . . . They burden themselves with images and rosaries which are showy and costly. . . . Others you will see adorned with medals and relics and tokens like children with trinkets. Here I condemn the attachment of heart . . . which is quite contrary to poverty of spirit, which considers only the sub-

stance of devotion and makes use only of what suffices for that end.[50]

Avarice begets the habit of acquiring not only things but also people. The avaricious person collects prestigious people as friends, acquiring autographs of the great and famous, entertains lavishly and, of course, takes care that none of this is unnoticed. Some parents push their children to extraordinary achievement, not for the children's sake but in order to show off their degrees or honors. Because the avaricious person has his heart set on things, he tends to reduce everything, including people, to the material level. He prices everything and values nothing.

Because avarice is a peculiarly earthbound sin, Dante has the covetous so bound and fettered that they can see nothing but the earth—the material things—upon which they have set their hearts. This shows how avarice debases all that is noble in human nature.

> What avarice works is known here as it is . . .
> For as our eyes would never seek the height,
> Being bent on earthly matters, earthward thus
> Justice here bends them in their own despite.[51]

Dante places in Purgatory not only those who love wealth but also Hugh Capet, punished for worldly ambition, and Pope Adrian V, characterized as being ambitious for ecclesial offices and honors.

Literature is full of misers, from Midas, whose golden touch delights him until it turns his daughter into a statue, to Dickens's Scrooge, denying the necessities and pleasures of life to others. In such characters the connection between "miser" and "miserable" is clear.

Jesus, too, tells parables that warn against avarice. The story of the fool who neglected his spiritual welfare in favor of building larger barns for greater wealth (Lk. 12:15-21) and the story of the rich man who ignored the beggar Lazarus at his door (Lk. 16:19-31) show how avarice closes the hearts of the greedy not only against other people but also against the kingdom of God. These rich men are so bound to finite things that the possibility of the infinite is irrevocably excluded.

Avarice thus enslaves the individual and warps or constricts his ability to love. A person is enslaved by what he loves; the more unworthy the object of love, the more shameful the slavery.

Avarice may be a direct sin against one's neighbor, either because the avaricious acquire unjustly or because they refuse to share with those in need. Thomas Aquinas observes that material goods, unlike spiritual things, cannot be possessed by many simultaneously. If one person has more, another has less, and if one has the whole pie, his neighbor is entirely deprived of it. Perhaps this is why Karl Menninger refers to the "sin of affluence," the global disparity which arises when one man has a billion dollars and a billion people have scarcely one dollar each.

The offspring of avarice include anxiety, hard-heartedness, loneliness, violence, theft, fraud and deceit.

The avaricious person can never be at peace; he can never acquire enough material goods nor possess them with sufficient security. He lives in constant fear lest "moth and rust consume and . . . thieves break in and steal" (Mt. 6:19). Such anxiety distracts— literally "tears apart"—the person who sets his heart on material things. His is poverty of spirit which is in sharp contrast to the recollectedness of a person whose interior powers are consolidated in a reserve of strength. The greater the inner lack, the more one needs to be propped up by exterior possessions.

Another child of avarice is hard-heartedness, a total lack of mercy and compassion. The miser can view the misery of others without mercy. He says, "People are in bread lines because they are too lazy to work. Giving to charity is contributing to indolence. Better the closed purse than the open heart." The miser is quick to point out fraud in poverty programs and slow to admit the existence of genuine need.

Because riches of the spirit tend to be inversely proportional to external wealth, the avaricious tend to be lonely. They have nothing to share but their wealth, and assuredly they will not share that. The pursuit of possessions has deprived them of the time to grow in the riches of mind and spirit, in care and concern for others. Thus they are unable to give themselves to others in friendship.

Violence, theft, fraud and deceit are other obvious children of avarice. The fact that many crimes begin with robbery and end with murder indicates that money is valued much more than human life.

The Old Testament proposes a very practical antidote to avarice: tithing. The people of God are to give God a tenth (tithe) of all they possess or earn. This is a way of admitting his sovereignty and their stewardship over earth's goods.

Contentment and gratitude work against avarice as well as envy; the section under the treatment of envy is also relevant here. Material things do not belong to human beings in an absolute way; they are God's gifts, and he can remove them, or life itself, as he sees fit. The person who sees his life as a gift from God and seeks to live it for God's glory does not measure his worth by what he possesses. Far from being enslaved by material things, he has the freedom to give them up for a greater good. He can exchange his Cadillac for a Honda, donate his Vermeer to an art gallery, and live in a cottage instead of a mansion without feeling less human or less happy. This does not mean he lacks appreciation for quality or beauty, only that his self-worth does not consist in the multiplicity of his possessions. He possesses them rather than being possessed by them.

> Fear not, little flock, for it is your Father's good pleasure to give you the kingdom. Sell your possessions, and give alms; provide yourselves with purses that do not grow old, with a treasure in the heavens that does not fail, where no thief approaches and no moth destroys. For where your treasure is, there will your heart be also (Lk. 12:32-34).

GLUTTONY

The Latin word for gluttony is *"gula"*: given a guttural pronunciation, it resembles the glutton's belch.

Gluttony is a disordered appetite for food or drink. It is not wrong to desire food. (As a matter of fact, to lack appetite for food and drink is another vice, called insensibility. One can commit this sin by failing to eat sufficient nourishing food or by failing to prepare it with care and beauty.) The desire for food becomes the sin of gluttony when it is disordered, leading to consumption of food for the wrong reason or in excess of one's needs. The glutton no longer eats to live; he lives to eat, and eating absorbs all his energies. A glutton can eat too much, eat the wrong things, or become preoccupied with food.

By "gluttony" most people mean eating more than one needs, more than one's belt or girdle can comfortably encompass, more often than one needs to eat (the habit of snacking). This kind of glutton finds no beauty in food. He does not care how delicately the food is prepared or presented, so long as there is plenty of it. He does not take time to taste or savor; he simply devours.

Excessive use of alcohol and drugs can also be the sin of gluttony. Psalm 104:15 lists among God's good gifts "wine to gladden the heart." The purpose of wine, then, is to gladden one's heart, not to besot the brain. (However, gluttony is not the only cause of excess in alcohol or drug usage. Many people use chemicals to dull physical or emotional pain, to escape responsibility or to stifle the constant gnawing of a purposeless life.)

Wasting food is another sin of gluttony. There has been a change in the American attitude toward food. As a child growing up on a farm, I was advised to take small portions and forced to finish all that I took, "Be careful; your eyes are bigger than your stomach. You're not leaving the table until you've eaten it all." Today, an amazing amount of food goes down the garbage disposal. Each day an average waitress carries out enough food on finished plates to feed a small village in India.

Another form of gluttony is eating the wrong things. In a country where food is abundant, many are poorly nourished. About 20% of every supermarket is filled with junk food and snacks containing little besides calories, laden with sugar or soaked in fat. How many children breakfast on sugary cereals, lunch on greasy hamburgers, snack on candy and potato chips, and wash it all down with pop? Although they eat constantly, they feel hungry and lack the energy to work well. Such children are allowed to indulge their preferences without any regard for nutrition.

A more refined form of gluttony is preoccupation with food and its preparation. The person whose beef must always be filet mignon, whose oysters must come from the Chesapeake Bay, and whose wine must be a $50 bottle of French burgundy is guilty of demanding delicacies. Delicacies are appropriate for a special occasion or feast; to eat only the rare and exotic betrays a gluttonous preoccupation with food.

Health-food addicts can be guilty of a similar gluttony, refusing to season with parsley unless it is organically grown, pouncing on every shred of evidence against potentially harmful methods of farming, preserving or packaging. Their interest in food and in their bodies is exaggerated and unnatural.

Spending excessive time seeking and preparing exotic foods is also gluttonous. This kind of glutton collects cookbooks and thumbs them for the exotic. He thinks, reads, worries and talks about food. His guests are regaled with detailed descriptions of ingredients, mode of preparation and final presentation. Thus the food which should sustain good conversation becomes the subject of conversation.

Dieters and calorie-counters can manifest a similar obsession with food, reading and thinking about it constantly. Their scales measure not pounds but ounces, and gaining a single ounce triggers a search for a more adequate diet. Of course, not every person suffering from overweight is a glutton; illness, stress, low metabolism and a host of other problems can cause a person to gain weight. In such cases, a strict diet may be very helpful. However, it should not become an end in itself.

Thus, contrary to our common stereotype, a person who eats very little can also be guilty of gluttony. For example, St. John of the Cross detects gluttony even in some forms of fasting:

> For many of these, lured by the sweetness and pleasure which they find in such exercises, strive more after spiritual sweetness than after spiritual purity and discretion. . . . The gluttony which they now have makes them continually go to extremes, so that they pass beyond the limits of moderation. . . . For some of these persons, attracted by the pleasure they find therein, kill themselves with penances, and others weaken themselves with fasts, by performing more than their frailty can bear. . . . But such one-sided penance is no more than the penance of beasts, to which they are attracted exactly like beasts, by the desire and pleasure which they find therein.[52]

As a capital sin, gluttony may lead to further sin. The person who indulges his appetite for sensual things will find his capacity for things of the mind and spirit dulled. He may fail to appreciate those witty remarks that spice a good dinner but rather interrupt a brilliant dinner conversation with loud guffaws or opt out of it with snores. Gluttony often prepares a person for the invasion of sloth or lust.

The gift of temperance or moderation may be better cultivated by considering the purpose of food in God's plan. Of course, food is intended to nourish the body, and a proper attention to this fact will reduce the influence of gluttony in snacking or eating junk food. Food is sacred because it supports life, and it becomes more sacred when it is blessed attentively. Grace should not be a mere formality but a way of expressing thanks, receiving food as one of God's good gifts to mankind. "Blessed are you, Lord God of all creation. Through your goodness we have this bread to eat." Occasional fasting helps heighten appreciation for food.

However, eating has a second purpose which is often over-looked, a social purpose. Eating for nourishment alone is an animal rather than a human activity, like hogs scrambling for the trough. Civilization has tried to dignify meals with plates and silver, linen and candles, and agreeable conversation; the purpose of etiquette is to make eating a more human and rational activity.

The Latin word for "banquet" is "*convivium*," which literally means "living together": a meal is the place where lives are welded together. Thus, food nourishes intimacy and community as well as the life of the individual. The first sin took place when Eve ate alone.

One can search the Gospels in vain for an occasion when our Lord ate alone. He prayed alone, he fasted alone, but there is no indication he ever ate alone. Even when he did the cooking, he waited until the Apostles came ashore (Jn. 21:9-13). The Gospels show Christ at many meals; the quality of the conversation there is conveyed by John 13-17.

Today many Christians do not know how to profit from the Eucharist because they do not understand or appreciate a meal. They come to the Eucharist with little or no preparation, receiving the body of Christ as they might receive a sandwich from an automat, with no time to linger and share after a good meal. This very individualistic approach overlooks the communal aspect of this most sacred meal. Christ said, "Abide in me, and I in you. As the branch cannot bear fruit by itself, unless it abides in the vine, neither can you, unless you abide in me. I am the vine, you are the branches" (Jn. 15:4-5). He did not say, "I am the vine and you are the branch," for he intended the Eucharist as the sacrament sustaining Christian community.

St. Paul's instructions on this matter also underscore the communal dimension of the Eucharistic meal. In 1 Corinthians 11:17-34, "discerning the body" means recognizing the real presence of Christ not primarily in the bread but especially in the believers gathered to share the Eucharistic meal.

LUST

The basic meaning of the English adjective "lusty" is strong or powerful. Thus one may speak of a lusty appetite for food and wine or a lusty battle cry. However, the noun "lust" is usually used to refer to the sexual drive (or another overwhelming passion, such as the lust for power).

As a capital sin, lust is sexual desire dominating a person in a way which is disordered, excessive, undisciplined or self-seeking. St. Isidore says the lustful person wallows in sensual pleasure.

Lust may mean the disordered use of sexuality. In this case, sexuality is good in being other-directed but disordered in being directed to the wrong person in the wrong circumstances (fornication). This seems to be the sense in which Dante uses lust. He puts the lustful at the highest cornice of Purgatory, where fire purifies these repentant sinners who "have loved not wisely but too well." Because he regards lust not as self-fascination but as the result of the impetus of excessive love, he finds it the least distorting and in need of the least purging.

However, lust more often refers to attachment to one's own sexual pleasure without regard for the good of one's sexual partner. As C.S. Lewis notes, "when a sex-starved sailor gets off a boat after a six months' cruise and says, 'I want a woman,' a woman is precisely what he doesn't want. He is not interested in personal relationship, but in an instrument of self-satisfaction."[53] The lustful person desires sensory pleasure, an event occurring within his own body. "Without [love], sexual desire, like every desire, is a fact about ourselves."[54] The paradigm of this sort of lust, of course, is masturbation, fixation on oneself as an object of pleasure.

We will focus on lust in this second sense, a fixation on self-gratification. For the first meaning we will use the term "sexual wrongdoing." Perhaps an example will clarify the distinction. Two people in love may genuinely desire to give themselves to each other sexually. If they are not married, this would be sexual wrongdoing, but it may not be lust. On the other hand, a married couple may stay together not because they love each other but because they derive so much sexual satisfaction from each other. There is no sexual wrongdoing in this case, but there may be deep and profound lust.

Although sexual wrongdoing may not begin in lust, it is not

thereby harmless. Good sexuality is so other-oriented that it is often mistaken for love. It frequently is an expression of love. However, if it is the only expression of love, it may in fact be self-love. Even genuine love that is not protected by commitment easily becomes inconstant, inconsiderate and superficial. When love is allowed to do what comes naturally, and only for as long as it comes naturally, that love fails to achieve a depth more profound than the erotic.

Ascetical theologians treat sexual pleasure with great caution for two reasons, its absorbing power and its basis in the sense of touch.

The sense of touch underlies the operation of all our senses. It is the last to become inactive when a person becomes unconscious and the first to return to awareness as he regains consciousness. (That is why it is so important to touch those who are unconscious or dying even when they are unable to speak or respond with anything but a hand-squeeze.) Because touch is so pervasive, it needs a great deal of discipline and control. The sense of touch can either be pampered or disciplined. Spiritual writers advise avoiding excess in food and drink, not surrounding the body with comforts: delightful smells, sensuous music, overly comfortable furniture or a sensuous environment. Rather, they recommend exercising wisely, partaking moderately of simple foods, enduring extremes of heat and cold, using firm beds and hard chairs. This does not mean becoming spartan or puritanical; it does recognize that pampered sensuality is the doorstep to lust. Disciplining the senses will help a person successfully resist the temptation to lust.

When spiritual writers warn how absorbing sexual pleasure is, they indicate its ability to hinder the effective exercise of the intelligence and will, to sabotage the best thoughts and decisions of a well-intentioned person.

Sexual desire is so strong that it often precipitates sin. Many sins—forging a check, cheating on taxes, misrepresenting items for sale, ruining another's reputation—are the products of deliberation. Sexual urges, on the other hand, come so spontaneously and so unbidden, with such tenacity and strength, that reflection and resistance seem almost overwhelmed from the start. That is why spiritual writers counsel precautions like modesty in dress and the avoidance of tempting situations: these strategies deal with the enemy "while the other is yet a great way off" (Lk. 14:32).

Why is the sexual urge so strong? As an urge human beings share with the animals, it is directly related to the preservation of the species, and that partially accounts for its strength. However, in human beings sexual desire is much more psychological than physical. Thought patterns, imagination, visual and other sensations are at least as stimulating as the sex drive itself, and in our society such stimuli are many. Finally, this area provides a vivid stage for the disorder sin has introduced into the human complex. The story of the first sin in Genesis indicates that some unruly stirrings were sensed as Adam and Eve became embarrassed at their nakedness.

Although lust is strong, its gratification is ephemeral. Jesus chooses his words carefully when he speaks of "lusting after" (Mt. 5:28). Lust is always in pursuit and ends as empty-handed as it began.

When sexuality is not infused with the spiritual, it quickly becomes boring; the multitude of sex manuals are an indication that this is exactly what is happening. Even worse, sexuality is taken to be the measure of one's entire life, and boredom with sex communicates itself to boredom with life as a whole.

One does not have to look far to find evidence of lust in our society. "People now seem to have sex on their minds," Malcolm Muggeridge once said, "which is a peculiar place to have it."[55] Lust is the theme of a large proportion of popular music, books and shows. Direct appeals to lust are used to sell everything from deodorant to automobiles. It has become fashionable to flaunt sexual wrongdoing. Vulgarities and obscene speech are in vogue, and they belch forth in public, leaving their fetid odor—in the form of graffiti—to decorate public places. "It is a humiliation of the flesh, of another's and of our own, and it is a perversity of our time that, in the name of a freedom that is delusive, we not only tolerate this humiliation but exalt it as a wonder of the modern age."[56]

Sexuality so treated loses its meaning. "A student who submitted himself to the inquiries of Alfred Kinsey said afterwards that, no matter what answer he gave to the questions, Kinsey just kept on asking him 'How many times?' Much in the same way, our society has reduced love to sex, sex to the act, and the act to merely a quantitative measure of it."[57]

St. John of the Cross writes of a certain spiritual eroticism that effectively weakens attachment to our Lord:

> Some of these persons make friendships of a spiritual kind with others, which often times is more erotic than spiritual in nature. This may be known to be the case when the remembrance of that friendship causes not the remembrance and love of God to grow, but occasions remorse of conscience. For, when the friendship is purely spiritual, the love of God grows with it; and the more the soul remembers it, the more it remembers the love of God, and the greater the desire it has for God.... If that sensual love grows, it will at once be observed that the soul's love of God is becoming colder, and that it is forgetting him as it remembers that love.[58]

The opposite of lust is chastity. Unfortunately, this word has come to have a negative and prudish connotation. Chastity is not the denial of sexuality. Rather, chastity subordinates sexuality to love, love of God and love of others. This means being willing to forego sexual pleasure in order to serve God or the other person. Even in marriage, sexuality is not an absolute right but one tool in love's workbox, not always the tool of choice. Chaste love seeks the beloved's greatest good and finds its own pleasure as the inevitable byproduct.

Sexual desire in the context of married love is directed toward the beloved. It is a mode of perception, which is why the Bible speaks of intercourse as a man "knowing" his wife (Gn. 4:9). Good sexuality is one expression of love, which has many other expressions, such as the gift of one's time, interest, service and self-sacrifice. Good sexuality is other-directed, relational. It builds a lasting unity between husband and wife which provides the foundation of their love and service to others.

In considering these seven deadly sins, we see that many of our human problems are caused directly by the flesh rather than the devil. On the other hand, the devil utilizes our individual weaknesses in these areas to turn us away from God. Discerning what is or is not Satan's influence in a specific immoral situation is a difficult but important task.

5. The Influences of Mental Illness

The field of psychology has had a great deal of experience in describing and classifying symptoms. In this chapter, we will draw on that expertise to describe mental/emotional disorders which are sometimes attributed to demonic influence. In the Middle Ages, such symptoms were usually blamed on the devil; in the 20th century, they are called mental illnesses. Taken categorically, both views are mistaken.

Bizarre behavior is not necessarily due to demonic influence. What follows are descriptions of patterns of behavior which, while strange and unusual, are often the result of psychological or physiological factors, not demonic. The point is to understand that these types of deviant behavior have been observed by science and their causes are somewhat understood. It would be wrong to assume Satanic influence was present, based simply on such behavior patterns.

To describe symptoms is not to determine their cause or to be able to effect a cure. Similar symptoms may be caused by emotional illness, by demon possession or by Satan exerting influence in an area of emotional weakness. It is as naive—and ineffective—to treat demon possession with medication and psychotherapy as it is to exorcise the mentally ill. In fact, as noted earlier, this may often exacerbate the problem. Hence discernment is of crucial importance, both the spiritual discernment and the discipline of diagnostic expertise.

A psychiatrist who also has a great deal of pastoral experience observes:

I personally have seen people with a diagnosis of schizophrenia who have been cared for with prayer, deliverance, strong supportive living situations, Christian teachings, etc., but without effect until the person took the proper medication. I have also seen someone who would have been called schizophrenic, but with love, care, strong support and prayer did very well without medication or direct psychiatric intervention. There were still problems, but not nearly to the degree one would have expected given the natural course of the illness. Discernment is a real key.

One should be cautious, unwilling to attribute a supernatural cause to something which may have a natural explanation. However, one should not rule out the possibility of actual demonic influence, as many modern theologians would do. Christians, who believe that each person has a spiritual nature and that the spiritual world is a reality, can never *a priori* rule out the possibility that the spiritual world can influence human persons.

Therefore, one cannot exclude the possibility of demonic influence, but neither should one be hasty in identifying it in a given case. Few people are possessed in the strict sense, and the cautions of the *Roman Ritual*, for example, are still full of wisdom. (Pére de Tonquedec admits that early in his ministry as official exorcist of the Diocese of Paris he went through the hospital exorcising patients, but with no observable results.)

Before attempting to relate the generally accepted classification of psychological illnesses to the possibility of demon possession, we will consider a few easily misused terms and several symptoms, such as hallucinations, which may occur in many different diseases.

The terms "neurosis" and "psychosis" describe the severity of mental illness in terms of the patient's perception of reality. The neurotic patient is aware that his symptoms are disproportional, maladaptive or otherwise distressing. The psychotic patient, on the other hand, is unable to do accurate reality testing. He is unaware that his perceptions or delusions or behavior do not correspond to objective reality and is unwilling to adjust them despite contrary evidence.

The psychotic person, for example, may firmly believe that he is the victim of an evil spirit or the chosen instrument of a brilliant spirit. In spite of appearances, this conviction does not rest upon ill will, pride, hatred or revenge; thus, religious or moral teaching will not motivate him to change it. Within him is a rock of conviction against which reasoning, insights, teachings and objections are broken and useless.

In itself this psychosis entails no general intellectual weakness, no other abnormal sensations or hallucinations. The person functions normally except in this particular area. He may be hyperlogical, subtle, insightful, acute in his powers of observation. However, he chooses and associates facts that are only tangentially related to the conclusion tenaciously imposed upon them.

If such a person seeks deliverance, he may insist that he is a victim: the devil orders his affairs, ruins his undertakings, affects his health, forces him to quit his profession, destroys his affections, breaks up his relationships.

Part of the evidence adduced for such interpretations may consist of **morbid dreams**: a person may dream that Satan is on his chest (incubus), that a demon is sucking out his life, that he is transported to a black mass or a witches' gathering. While the devil can certainly influence the imagination and insert himself into dreams, such dreams in themselves need not indicate possession; they are what I referred to in Chapter 3 as ordinary temptations. The problem occurs when the dreamer becomes convinced of the reality of his dreams, perhaps pointing out self-inflicted scratches or bites which he blames on witches or demons.

A person suffering from neurosis may discover prophetic warnings in his dreams and be paralyzed by fear of their fulfillment. For example, a young man who dreamed he would die at 30 postponed marriage until 31 for fear of leaving a widow and young children.

Like dreams, perceptions and hallucinations can be taken as evidence of demonic activity or can be confused with reality.

Hallucination is not the same as daydreaming, where a person sees himself in heroic roles but is aware that this is the product of imagination and wishful thinking. In hallucination, he perceives as external to himself something that others cannot verify. He may hear one or more voices speaking to him, report ominous noises (footsteps, furniture moving, windows being slammed), see sinister figures (lights, phantoms, the devil with blazing eyes or under bestial appearance), report physical sensations (a snake in his abdomen) or smell fetid odors. He may sense the presence of someone or something in the room. He may perceive things ranging from the everyday to the bizarre.

When someone reports such manifestations, it is important to question him further: What action does the individual feel is necessary in response to the voice or the hallucination? If the voice commanded him to jump out a window, is he planning on responding to this command? Who else witnessed these phenomena? What is their mental and emotional state? If several people were witnesses, have they been examined separately to eliminate the possibility of group suggestion?

Even if the events are verifiable, and not the result of hallucination, one should not assume a supernatural explanation for something that could have a natural explanation. For example, I once lived in an old house whose boards would creak in the middle of the night as if someone were walking along the hallway. Since investigation revealed no one, I could easily have supposed a phantom. However, I came to understand that it was a progressive contraction of the beams which began closest to the exterior wall and was transmitted the length of each beam. In other cases, the perception has an external cause but one which is barely perceptible. For example, a slight draft or alternation of shadows in a dark room can suggest the presence of something evil.

Some things which frequently cause hallucinations are specific physical illnesses (including head injury, seizure, infection, high fever and metabolic imbalance) and certain medications. Besides such external phenomena as hallucinations, a person may experience more internal **obsessions** such as the forceful injection of ideas, images, interior attitudes or phrases. Horrible and indecent spectacles flash through the person's mind and he cannot seem to be rid of them. He may experience and evidence in his appearance sentiments of hatred, contempt or insolence which he himself detests, or he may feel impelled to commit evil acts.

People sometimes mistakenly attribute such phenomena to the devil; they may also mistakenly adduce human or natural causes such as mental telepathy or communication from another person, living or dead. These obsessive ideas are not the same as flashes of intuition or conviction that do not seem to rest on a conscious reasoning process. Such flashes of insight are seldom attributed to the devil, because they are not associated with evil or repugnant images and activities.

It is very difficult to establish whether such obsessions spring from diabolic influence or from one's sinful or subconscious being. A spiritual diagnosis is more probable in the case of violent disturbance, vehement impulses to evil, and the presence of other manifestations associated with the diabolic. The ineffectiveness of purely medical or psychiatric treatment can be another clue. There are many organically caused diseases which have psychological manifestations. These should not be mistaken for mental disorder or demonic activity. Here we might include dementia and epilepsy, and perhaps substance abuse would be a further extension of this category, since psychological symptoms can be precipitated by drugs.

Alzheimer's disease is one common example of **dementia**; this affects memory and other mental abilities, impulse control, and the ability to care for oneself and to relate to other people normally. In dementia, personality changes are due to such factors as aging, brain disease or injury.

Epilepsy is an organic disease with psychological side-effects. It includes not only grand mal seizures, in which loss of consciousness, rigidity and muscle spasms are clear indications of the attack, but also petit mal seizures, in which loss of consciousness is so partial or temporary that the victim and those around him may not be aware that anything has happened. The patient may appear to be conscious and purposeful but has no later recollection of his actions.

While few people would mistake a grand mal seizure for demon possession, demons can mimic epilepsy. (See Matthew 17:14-18.) Furthermore, epileptics may experience hallucinations or other unusual sensations and have post-seizure impulses to violence, arson or sexual attack. This is usually not purposeful violence but nondirected aggression or a lessened ability to tolerate frustration, which predisposes epileptics to outbursts of rage.

Symptoms of petit mal may easily be mistaken for phenomena of the spirit world. Besides slight physical symptoms such as movement of the fingers, a gentle weaving of the body, blinking of the eyes, pallor and a vacant stare, a person experiencing a petit mal seizure may speak incoherently or obscenely, attack those around him, destroy objects, or tear his clothes. He may be seized with a violent and inexplicable outburst of anger. This can suggest demonic influence, especially if the person is moved to attack religious objects or refuses to go to church.

The after-effects of a petit mal attack may last for hours or even days and may include manic behavior and an eclipse of the person's moral sense. Such a person suffers no hallucinations and shows no trace of mental confusion; he seems to be reasoning lucidly, yet he plunges into wrongdoing, boasts about it, seems to revel in it. He may be well-educated and cultured, and the wrongdoing which tempts him would normally be totally repugnant to him: gross blasphemy, revolt against God, insults to priests and religious, impure acts even in the presence of others.

In some seizure victims, particularly those whose conditions have been poorly treated, personality development is significantly influenced. This is complicated when the onset of seizures in a child's life is met by negative attitudes of family and society. Poor social adjustment sometimes leads to antisocial and criminal behavior.

Although an epileptic seems to have two personalities at war with each other, this does not indicate demon possession, and exorcism is ineffective.

We now turn to mental disorders which do not seem to be organically caused but rather the result of psychological processes. We will highlight those which are most easily mistaken for demonic possession.

Somatoform disorders include somatization disorder (the patient has recurrent multiple complaints), psychogenic pain disorder (pain which seems to be psychologically rather than physically caused), hypochondriasis (the patient interprets minor symptoms as abnormal and is convinced that he has some fatal disease). We will focus on a fourth type, conversion disorder, in which the patient acts as if he is paralyzed, blind or otherwise afflicted although there is no organic cause.

For our purposes **factitious disorders** operate in a similar fashion. The patient with this diagnosis manifests physical or psychological illness, but it seems to be somewhat voluntary; that is, his symptoms exacerbate when he knows he is being observed, and he is very suggestible about assuming additional symptoms. However, like the person with a conversion disorder, he is not simply putting on an act, and he is not conscious of the inner needs which are being served by his illness.

Two mechanisms have been suggested to explain what the individual derives from having a conversion symptom. In one, the individual achieves "primary gain" by keeping an internal conflict or need out of his awareness. For example, after an argument, inner conflicts about the expression of rage may be expressed in the inability to speak or move one's arm. These symptoms have symbolic value that represents and partially solves the unyielding psychological conflict.

In the other mechanism, the individual achieves "secondary gain" by avoiding a particular activity that is noxious to him or by getting support from the environment that otherwise might not be forthcoming. For example, with a "paralyzed" hand a soldier can avoid firing a gun; with "blindness" a very dependent person may try to ensure that his spouse will not desert him.

Conversion disorder may be precipitated by some traumatic event: an illness or injury or some other stressful occurrence or conflict. If the patient is able to face the problem or bring the conflict into consciousness, his symptoms will usually disappear.

Personality disorders are distinguished from personality traits by the fact that they are inflexible and maladaptive. Everyone has characteristic patterns of perceiving, relating to and thinking about the environment and himself, but the person with a personality disorder behaves in ways that cause him distress or impair his ability to function socially or occupationally. One group of personality disorders lead to odd or eccentric behavior. These include paranoid disorder (the person who is convinced someone—or everyone—is trying to destroy him) and schizoid disorder (the person who is unable to relate to others because he seems unaware of their feelings or his own). Another group of personality disorders are erratic, dramatic and emotion-laden. These include histrionic disorder (the person who is intense and excitable about everything), narcissistic disorder (the person who demands attention and success and becomes enraged if he fails or is ignored by others), and antisocial disorder (manifested in lying, stealing, fighting, sexual abuse and inability to respect authority or hold a job).

Some combination of histrionic and narcissistic personality disorders may explain the behavior of a group of pseudomiracle-workers, pseudoprophets, visionaries, false converts (who love to reenact all the details of their conversion before an audience), and founders of sects whose oracles rule their credulous disciples. Among these people may be found all degrees of sincerity and falsehood. Often they possess such genuine virtue that one feels they could not be guilty of deliberate deceit. (In testing their claims, one must exert strict control so that they do not in fact trick one.)

Other victims of similar personality disorders may take on quite the opposite characteristics. They attract attention to themselves by acting repulsively or by alternating roles of holiness and diabolic possession, portraying themselves as chosen souls exposed to exceptional trials and favored with exceptional graces. Such individuals may truly seem to be possessed, but formal exorcism only reenforces the dominating idea. In such cases, I prefer to pray with the person in English for healing and to pray an exorcism in Latin; the devil understands Latin quite well, and if there is an evil spirit his presence will become known.

A third group of personality disorders are manifested by anxious and fearful people. These include avoidant disorder (the person who is so afraid of being rejected that he withdraws), compulsive disorder, passive-aggressive disorder and dependent disorder. We will discuss the last three in more detail.

The person with a **compulsive personality disorder** is a perfectionist whose devotion to productivity excludes pleasure. He is so preoccupied with rules, efficiency and trivial details that he cannot grasp the big picture. He avoids decision-making for fear of making a mistake and often falls short of his own ideals. He has trouble expressing warm and tender feelings and tends to be excessively conscientious, scrupulous and judgmental of self and others. When unable to control others, he becomes angry but does not express this directly; rather, he may become depressed, hypochondriac or obsessive-compulsive. (See the discussion of obsessive-compulsive behavior later in this chapter, under anxiety disorders.)

The person with a **passive-aggressive personality disorder** resists demands that he perform adequately, but his resistance is indirectly expressed in procrastination, inefficiency or forgetfulness. This seems to be a continuation of adolescent oppositional disorder.

The person with a **dependent disorder** lets others assume responsibility for major areas of his life. He has so little self-esteem that he dares make no demands on others lest they desert him. This person may be very suggestible. Like soft wax capable of receiving any impression, he repeats words, gestures and attitudes he observes in others. He may engage in such behavior as automatic writing, inscribing messages he readily believes come from the beyond, since their content astonishes him. It is easy to see how such a person might come to believe himself possessed, although the so-called messages actually come either from within himself (unrecognized needs) or from other people upon whom he is dependent. People with dependent disorders readily believe themselves to be under spells or charms. I once dealt with a young man from Africa who claimed to be under a spell from a witch in his African tribe who was exerting magical influence to kill him. This young man used to come periodically for a half-gallon of holy water which he used faithfully, but there was no response to a number of silent exorcisms which I prayed. Such simple people are victims of suggestion, not demons. However, the power of suggestion can be so strong that people have been known to die from such spells.

Schizophrenic disorders involve delusions, hallucinations and thought disturbances. They so affect the person that he is unable to care for himself, relate to others or do his work.

Schizophrenics commonly manifest disordered thought and speech: ideas shift from one subject to an unrelated one without the speaker being aware of any incoherence. Schizophrenic delusions may include the belief that others are plotting to harm the individual (persecutory delusions) and the belief that alien feelings, thoughts and actions are being imposed upon him (delusions of being controlled). The schizophrenic may be confused about his own identity and seem out of touch with his own feelings. He finds it difficult to make decisions or pursue a goal and may even become catatonic, unresponsive to everything around him. This can easily be mistaken for demon possession, but on closer examination it will be found to have deep roots in the person's development and experiences.

Paranoid disorders involve persistent delusions of being persecuted. The paranoid may be jealous and violent, but he is generally lucid and in touch with reality in every other area, unlike the schizophrenic. If the paranoid feels persecuted by superhuman evil forces, he is likely to believe himself harassed by the devil, yet exorcism will only strengthen his conviction of being persecuted rather than free him from such harassment.

Affective disorders are mood disturbances, severe emotional states that color a person's whole psychological life. The common types are bipolar disorder (with alternating manic and depressive episodes) and major depression.

In the manic phase, the person is expansive, euphoric, hyperactive, distractible and/or irritable. He may talk constantly, express grandiose delusions, and engage in impulsive actions (buying sprees, reckless driving, sexual orgies) with no consideration of their consequences. Such manic states may alternate with depression but rarely if ever exist without depression; it is as if the person must later punish himself for his manic excesses.

In a major depressive episode, the person feels fatigued and disinterested. Gloomy days ooze away without brightness in an atmosphere of malaise. He seems bent down by a burden impossible to lift, a prey to nightmares from which he never awakens. Convinced of his worthlessness, he may neglect himself or try to end his life, though his attempts can be half-hearted.

Some depressed persons behave quite differently, manifesting great anxiety. Their gestures, their movements, their walk manifest restlessness, impatience, suffering. They affect humble postures, refuse to be seated, lower their heads, invent ineffectual means of expiating their faults, inflict wounds on themselves, refuse to eat, anticipate new blows of fortune and ventilate their fears. They are talkative, but their conversation is limited to their bad luck.

The cause of this sadness is vague and undefined, although it may be a delayed or recurrent reaction to some past event such as the loss of a loved one. Another depressed person may be laden with guilt feelings for general wrongdoing, attributing unheard-of consequences to specific sins: "My sins have brought God's curse down on my family, caused earthquakes in Turkey, starvation in the Sahara. My sins are so great there is no hope; I shall surely go to hell."

Because the depressed person feels so worthless and guilt-laden, he or those around him may easily attribute his suffering to the devil. How could he have such sinful feelings—hatred of God, repulsion for religion—unless he had given way to the devil? "God must now be rejecting and punishing me for my unforgivable sins."

The person who is genuinely possessed may manifest hatred of God and a sense of his own damnation. However, the possessed person does not usually manifest this kind of depression (always in tears, anxious and fearful, with a taste for nothing and no interest in taking care of himself). Furthermore, the possessed person usually alternates sadness or feelings of damnation with normal states, whereas the depressed person is always in possession of himself. It is he who is guilty, who accuses himself, who feels damned.

Depression is more like certain trials of the dark night of the spirit, in which the person being purified experiences a weighty sense of his own sinfulness and abandonment by God. Such a person may lose his taste for everything and feel he can neither repair the damage done by his sins nor have recourse to the mercy of God. Such spiritual trials can be distinguished from major depressive episodes by the profound difference in the person's overall orientation. A person enters the dark night in the course of his journey toward God, earnestly desiring to do God's will even when every emotional consolation is removed.

Anxiety is a strong and unpleasant sense of apprehension, often accompanied by physiological symptoms. **Anxiety disorders** include phobia (persistent irrational fear which motivates a person to avoid a specific object, act or situation), anxiety states (panic attacks or extreme apprehensiveness with no specific cause), and obsessive-compulsive disorder, which we will consider in greater detail. Anxiety disorders may be precipitated by a traumatic experience (war, rape, torture) or may be rooted more deeply in the personality. It should also be noted that certain physical illnesses and medications may mimic anxiety states.

In obsession, recurrent ideas or images are experienced not as voluntary but as invading the person from outside. In compulsion, apparently purposeful acts—such as counting, touching, (automatic) writing or hand-washing—are repeated in an excessive or unrealistic way. If the person tries to resist such a compulsion, he becomes increasingly tense and anxious. The flip side of compulsion is inhibition: a person seems prevented from doing what he wants to do.

These compulsions may be sexual in nature, such as compulsions to masturbation or erotic encounters. People with such compulsions may fight against them, sometimes yield to them, then be filled with remorse. These temptations themselves can stir up strong guilt feelings. One young man felt very guilty about evil actions he feared he might commit; at times he felt like committing the actions just to see if the guilt would go away.

Everyone experiences this sort of phenomenon: a song keeps

running through one's head, a singular expression keeps coming to mind. However, the person with an obsessive-compulsive disorder is dominated by his obsession, and its emotional impact is powerful. For example, a person who had a traumatic experience as a child may constantly see the image of a man dangling from a rope, or constantly hear the cries of a child trapped in a burning building. Often this obsessive idea leads to compulsive behavior. A person is afraid to light a match lest the house catch fire, feels the urge to hang himself whenever he sees a rope, or washes his hands incessantly in a vain attempt to dispel infection.

Many people with this psychological disorder find themselves doing the opposite of what they want to do. For example, they wish to receive the Eucharist but feel impelled to profane it. They pick up the Bible only to find themselves laughing at what they read. This behavior makes them feel very guilty, and they may seek to discover events in their past which might possibly explain this evil influence.

These are usually people of unstable temperament. They are besieged by fears, and the fear of doing certain things so fascinates them that they seem driven to do those very things. For example, one man who has a great fear of heights experiences a strong impulse to jump whenever he reaches a certain height. So powerful is this force that he will not go above this height unless accompanied by another person who can restrain him if the compulsion becomes overwhelming.

How can it happen that a person feels driven to do the opposite of what he desires or chooses?

Some people seem driven to contradict others: if someone says the sky is blue, they will counter by saying, "That is not the sky, and it's red." This is not always the product of perverseness, rebelliousness, antipathy or the desire to be noticed. It can be immediate and instinctive, a sort of mental tic.

Some people contradict not only others but themselves. No thought can present itself to them without immediately arousing its opposite. When this contradiction in thought invades the field of action, a person feels himself compelled to do the opposite of what he wishes to do, or of what is suggested to him.

If the person with this malady is a religious person, it is not surprising to find him losing his grip on the faith which means so much to him. He is so attached to this faith and so fearful of losing it that his very attachment evokes its opposite. The idea of apostasy presents itself. He seeks to resolve his doubts by reflecting on faith's foundations, by arousing hatred for his doubts. This causes even more difficulties. Lacking mental equilibrium, he cannot reflect calmly or reason to the cause of his difficulties. He may even become an apostate, rejecting everything he once believed so tenaciously.

Many experience these difficulties at Holy Communion, the most sacred action of their religious practice. They find themselves unable to swallow the host or, worse, are moved to profane it. Blasphemous thoughts besiege them and are sometimes uttered in spite of themselves. Scrupulosity is frequently an example of this kind of compulsion: a person longs to live free from sin yet is obsessed by the impression that he has committed a terrible sin.

Thus the very intensity of one's devotion can beget its opposite, dominating the consciousness and behavior of the mentally ill person. Note that blasphemy or sacrilege is only one form of oppositional compulsion. A more secular example would be the devoted mother who feels impelled to take a knife and cut the throats of her children, but is terrified lest she actually do this.

People who are prey to such compulsions and inhibitions readily entertain the idea that they are possessed by some external force, especially if they feel compelled to do something morally wrong.

It is quite possible that Satan may be tempting individuals through such natural weaknesses. However, these obsessions and compulsions in themselves do not point to an evil agent just because they are concerned with matters of religion or morality. Whatever is very important to a person may become a source of inhibitions or compulsions. For example, a doctor whose patient dies may become so frightened that he is unable to treat other patients, just as a religious person may fear to approach the Eucharist. On a more trivial level, a mathematician may feel compelled to add the numbers on every license plate to determine whether the sum is odd or even and whether it is a prime number.

The person with an obsessive-compulsive disorder feels that he is no longer in control of his actions; from this experience, he may conclude that someone else—such as the devil—is controlling him.

His actions seem purposeful, yet they do not express his purposes, hence he is convinced that someone else is using him as an instrument. He rightly understands the psychological reality: he is not free. However, he wrongly concludes to a demonic cause. The cause lies rather within his own psyche.

Impulse control disorders include pathological gambling, stealing and arson. Another form is intermittent explosive disorder, in which the person occasionally seems to lose control of his aggressive impulses. He may later feel guilty and accept responsibility for his actions, yet he feels compelled from beyond himself.

A **dissociative disorder** is a sudden temporary change in consciousness, identity or behavior. These disorders include the familiar amnesia (loss of memory) and multiple personality (the existence of two or more distinct and often conflicting personalities, with sudden transitions from the dominance of one to the dominance of another). In a depersonalization disorder, the person feels estranged from himself, perhaps mechanical or unreal.

It is easy to mistake a dissociative disorder such as multiple personality for diabolic possession. Perhaps it would be helpful to consider what sort of persons manifest such symptoms and what may precipitate the illness.

Consider an individual of no great intellectual or critical ability, perhaps somewhat lacking in common sense, who is dominated by his imagination and does not readily distinguish the imaginary from the real. He may permit himself to be guided by his imagination and begin to live his images, imitating the gestures, attitudes and actions of the people or things he imagines. Because he does this almost instinctively, it is difficult to distinguish this person from someone deliberately putting on an act. Perhaps it is not a matter of black and white but of half-truth, of little blows given more or less consciously to the integrity of the truth, softening it up to make it more like one's secret desires. Such a person cannot see himself as he is. He is only intermittently lucid with respect to himself and cannot distinguish dream from reality.

Thus, when reality no longer corresponds to the individual's aspirations, he takes flight into a dream-life which can deform reality and eventually supplant it. Although the new "reality" (multiple personalities, for example) seems discontinuous with the person's previous character, on deeper examination it will be found to express subconscious needs, desires, anxieties or conflicts.

While many of these psychological illnesses suggest demonic influence, there are differences, which can be detected by a trained counselor or experienced pastor. These differences frequently emerge when the person is questioned about his background and about when his present difficulties first became apparent.

Discernment must combine careful analysis with prayer and fasting. It is not a matter of plugging information into a computer and coming out with an infallible diagnosis; rather, one must rely on the Holy Spirit to reveal the hidden needs, desires and conflicts of the human heart, distinguishing what lies within the person himself and what has invaded him from the demonic realm.

6. Methods for Discernment and Deliverance Prayer

The pastoral approach in this book assumes that Satan is a wily general who attacks human beings in the areas of their greatest weakness. Thus, we have considered the capital sins because they are the fonts of spiritual weakness, along with some varieties of mental or emotional disorder or weakness. We have spent less time on purely physical illnesses because such illnesses in themselves are not usually the main thrust of Satan's attack; he merely uses physical complaints as a means to attack us in other areas: spiritual, emotional or mental.

I have further indicated that there are not, strictly speaking, many cases of actual possession by a demonic spirit. Possession is somewhat grotesque in its exhibition and it may actually turn observers against Satan. His interest certainly lies in drawing people to himself, so he normally chooses more subtle, undercover means to achieve his purposes.

The person with pastoral responsibility needs discernment and intelligence to determine, if possible, some useful purpose behind Satan's actions or some possible goal he may have in mind. By understanding his strategies, we can better oppose his actions. This does not mean that we shall always be able to uncover what he is doing, since his intelligence is greater than ours and his designs more far-reaching. It does seem that part of his plan is, for whatever reason, to multiply smaller-scale occasions of temptation, harassment, intimidation and fear, rather than to concentrate on actually gaining possession of people. Thus, there seems to be much greater need for the prayer of deliverance than for exorcism.

Deliverance takes two forms. In the first, the minister, pastoral leader or the person in charge invokes the power of God in an authoritative way, that is to say, deliverance is a command made by a Christian exercising the authority of Jesus Christ. Jesus is the Lord of the person under attack. Deliverance first reminds the devil of this fact and then orders him to lift his siege of this person and to depart from this territory upon which he has encroached. In the name of Jesus and as his representative, the Christian believer commands Satan to depart and to surrender this territory again to its rightful Lord and king.

A slightly different method of deliverance is a prayer addressed to God. Any of us can ask the Lord to set someone free from the influence of various temptations and harassments which come from evil spirits. This may happen either in the presence of the one afflicted or in his absence. The evil spirit is not addressed or commanded directly.

Prayer is more effective, of course, when a group of Christians gathers with the person who needs to be set free, because there is often a need for counseling, discernment and encouragement as well as for prayer itself. In the following pages I will offer a format for this kind of group prayer, which has proven successful in hundreds of examples of demonic interference.

Pastorally, I think it may be wise to be a little loose in the process of coming to an understanding of the chief problems. I don't think it is all that useful to concentrate on each and every symptom, calculating what may be demonic and what psychological, what is natural and what is supernatural and so forth. Our approach should not be either/or but both/and. The overriding concern is for the person being prayed for. It is quite all right to "cover all the bases," praying specifically whenever possible, but also praying generally to take care of whatever we might have missed or misunderstood. Earthly, heavenly and infernal influences commingle in all of us. In some ways the most important thing is that God is Lord of all these influences, rather than that we understand each in its correct proportion.

In deliverance—as in all counseling, spiritual direction and inner works of the Spirit—there is a common theme: the person's confrontation with what may be considered weaknesses or failures. The person has a sense, perhaps inchoate, that there is something wrong or amiss. The person will likely be hesitant to expose or to confront what is wrong, and thus half the battle may be against an understandable fear or anxiety. For this reason, it is clear that any attempt to pray for deliverance must occur in an atmosphere of acceptance, confidence, encouragement, support and love. The tone should not be one of tense, fearful uneasiness, but one of confident and assured victory.

Some have noted that Scripture itself makes no distinction among what we would distinguish as varying degrees of possession, extent of demonic interference, types of harassment and so on. The authors record Jesus dealing with *all* demonic activity by means of a simple command, or with the additional recommendation of "prayer and fasting" (Mk. 9:29). Thus, we know that in our search for wisdom in this process we must never forget the simple fact of Jesus' lordship and the power he demonstrates when we pray. We can't allow our own efforts—well-intentioned as they are—to distract us from the primary truth that it is by God's power and authority that Satan is routed.

Initial contact with someone who might be suffering from demonic harassment usually comes from a third party. Perhaps the troubled person comes into personal contact with another Christian who knows what deliverance is about. Perhaps a pastor, psychiatrist or psychologist or an acquaintance has observed some bizarre behavior and senses that it might involve the demonic. If the referral is a professional one, a discussion with the psychiatrist or psychologist will introduce the minister or pastoral leader to the facts of the case. It is important to determine whether a problem is simply a mental one rather than demonic. If there is no evidence of the demonic, great care should be exercised because of the sometimes extreme suggestibility of people needing medical care. Bringing up the existence of the devil can cause more confusion, not less.

There are several questions to be asked in the process of discernment. In the simplest case, the individual is normally well-balanced and manages his life quite well. He will be able to give accurate and even objective descriptions of his state of mind when he is not himself. There is a decided contrast between his ordinary frame of mind and the exceptional state induced by . . . whatever.

First, ask whether the person has had any dealings with the occult, or whether the person's family has ever been known to delve into the occult. Even the common forms such as ouija boards should be included here. It is also important to know whether addictive drugs or consciousness-altering materials have been used in the past or present and to what extent. The leader should be especially alert for statements which indicate attitudes which are congenial to demonic initiative: "I'd do anything to get that money," "My life is out of control." Newspaper horoscopes are not in the same category with witchcraft, but an avid attention to them indicates a weakness which a demon could use.

In asking these questions, it is best to be direct and blunt, but not threatening. At this stage, information is simply being sought.

Second, consider a brief medical history. Determine whether the person or any member of his immediate family has ever been under psychiatric or psychological care. If so, ascertain the nature of the illness and its treatment. If the person himself is currently under professional care, proceed only with the knowledge and approval of the professional person.

Third, determine whether the person genuinely wants to be set free from the evil influence and from all attachment to it. More on this point later.

With this kind of background in place, discernment proceeds. Prayer for insight and enlightenment is important, but consideration of the person's history provides some direct indications. If, for example, there is no evidence of medical problems, but there has been experience of the occult and the person really wants to be free, then the decision is clear: proceed with scheduling a deliverance session.

Demonic interference in a person's life may not be obvious— either to the person himself or to the pastoral leader. There are some instances in which the signs of trouble are less obvious. Perhaps a person notes simply the presence in himself of major obstacles or blocks to Christian growth in the process of spiritual direction, counseling, healing of memories, inner healing or the sacrament of Reconciliation. The person notes little success in spite of determined effort in an area of weakness. Perhaps he senses a compulsion to wrong behavior. He is tempted fiercely, insistently, almost constantly.

Here, a clear possibility is that a demon is manipulating a weakness of character or a moral weakness to undercut the person's growth in Christ. This has not resulted in anything that could be regarded as supernaturally bizarre or too much out of the ordinary. Rather, it appears to be a rather extreme example of the normal temptations and attacks we are all subject to. The intensity and/or frequency have brought the person to the point where the prayer of deliverance may well cause a breakthrough of grace which has not been possible through normal daily prayer.

The minister or pastoral leader should suggest to the person in these situations that the prayer of deliverance is available and recommended. If the person agrees, schedule a time when a small group can gather. I suggest that the sessions last not longer than two hours each, nor more than about two weeks apart. I say this simply because this kind of prayer can be very demanding. Both he who prays and he who is delivered can be liable to suggestion or manipulation because of fatigue.

Sometimes one session of prayer will be enough. Often, however, if the influence is deep-seated or of long duration, several sessions will be necessary. The person ought not be discouraged at the end of a session if it appears that little has been accomplished or that much remains to be done. This is normal. Also, the person should know that the limited time available in the prayer session does not limit the work of God. Very often the Lord will accomplish things in-between prayer sessions or after the series has been completed.

Some years ago I led a team in prayer of deliverance for a middle-aged woman. We prayed with her several times; very little seemed to have happened. Yet the third time she returned for prayer she expressed complete freedom from the oppression she had been suffering. This kind of prayer perdures. I have seen many people delivered several days following deliverance sessions.

Before praying, be sure that the person genuinely desires to be free of the evil influence. It does happen that a person can become emotionally attached to it. As bizarre as this may seem, it is understandable. The evil influence and the struggle against it have become part of the fabric of life. The person may have adjusted to the influence, especially if it is entangled with some character flaw. The person may have become comfortable with the status quo. He may feel that the situation is like an amputation—one wills the diseased member to be severed but hates to see it go. There is a real importance in the renunciation of Satan and all his allurements. The person should understand that this renunciation includes all emotional attachments as well.

There is room for a great deal of pastoral flexibility in this kind of prayer. Gathering a group of people together is better, but there are fine reasons to limit the session to three people. One can hardly do with fewer than three: the person to be prayed for, the leader and one other person who can pray constantly or give the leader a rest when there is need to do so. It is essential that a woman be present on the team if a woman is being prayed for.

All members of the team—and most especially the leader— must be embued with an unshakeable faith. Men and women of moral integrity, spiritual wisdom and maturity in the Christian life must make up the overwhelming majority of team members. I say "overwhelming majority" because the person being prayed for may request that a personal friend or spouse also be present at the session as an observer.

All team members should be fortified sacramentally, according to the opportunities afforded by their respective denominations. Whether they are team members on a regular basis or for only one session, they must be persons capable of protracted prayer, persons of fearless disposition. Evil spirits capitalize on weaknesses, known or unknown, so team members must be strong and forthright, confident and grounded in a personal closeness to the Lord Jesus.

The leader ought to have attended several sessions of this type, if possible, before undertaking to lead one. More than anyone else, he should typify the team's confident faith and reliance on the Lord while confronting the evil spirits with the conquering strength of God. The leader should have a strong constitution, and arrive at the session prepared to do battle. Obviously, the leader must be a person of solid Christian belief and practice, genuinely charitable and highly motivated, humble and reverential.

It is not necessary that anyone on the team have personally experienced any diabolic manifestations. Prior personal experiences of such afflictions may or may not be beneficial at the session, depending on the individual case. Team members should be chosen on other grounds than this.

The tone of the session is very important and should be under the influence of the leader. There should be no hint of desperation, of hopelessness, of fatigue, of superciliousness or of negative emotions or moods. An easygoing confidence in the power of God, a simple and direct faith, a complete trust in God's overcoming power and in his love will contribute mightily to the progress of the session. The leader should be obviously in command, should never shirk responsibility or fail to exercise authority when necessary.

The word "deliverance" evokes images of freedom from bondage or release from prison, but other metaphors are also appropriate and should be invoked, in particular that of a spiritual battle or campaign, with warriors ready to fight the battle and to win.

The leader should offer a few instructions to the person who is to be prayed with before the prayer actually begins. He should liken the prayer session to young David's killing of Goliath with merely a slingshot, or to the Hebrews being rescued from their pursuers at the Red Sea, or to whatever other scriptural parallels suggest themselves. Passages from Scripture should be read at any time during the session, at the discretion of the leader.

Note that there are "two or three gathered together" in the name of Jesus, so that he is present (Mt. 18:20). Jesus promised that he would be present in such situations, and he is faithful to his promise. The name of Jesus should not be omitted, and in fact should be used often, rather than constantly using the titles of Jesus, such as Lord, Christ, Savior and the like. Proclaim the personal name of Jesus throughout the session along with his titles. There is divine power present where the name of Jesus is spoken, and experience recommends this practice very specifically.

Encourage the person being prayed for, that is, call forth an attitude of courageous effort and determination. Call to the person's attention that he or she is not alone, that there are other prayer warriors about, along with numerous angels eager to do battle, with all enveloped in the love and power of Jesus Christ himself, present through his Holy Spirit. If the person expresses any sense of fear, perhaps it would be good to pray quickly for release from that fear before proceeding.

The leader should speak in a normal voice, even conversationally, when addressing the person being prayed for. It is best to use a translation of Scripture in modern English.

I have classified deliverance prayer into six steps. I believe these are the basic requirements, and others may be added as the occasion demands.

STEP ONE: Humility

The leader should speak to the person to be prayed for and encourage an attitude of humility, based on the realization of who

God is, who human beings are, and who Satan is. Words such as the following may be used:

> God is the Creator and we and Satan are all his creatures. Evil spirits exist under the authority of God. Satan's plan is that he turn us away from God, teaching us either to rely upon ourselves or upon himself rather than the Lord. In times of temptation, we are being tested so that we can be proven faithful to God in all things.
>
> God is objectively real, the greatest spiritual power in the universe and even beyond. God is Lord of everything and of every creature. God desires our utter faithfulness to him. He is with us in strength to protect us, to deliver us, to set us free. God knows every hair on our heads. We can imagine ourselves on a seashore with the limitless horizon stretching away before us, knowing that we are very small in the context of the whole of creation, yet also knowing that we are chosen by God out of love to be his children. God is on our side, and we can depend on him rather than on our own spiritual strength, which would not be enough to stand against Satan indefinitely. We have nothing to be afraid of because our strength is the Lord.
>
> The people on the prayer team have the discernment to pray for the Lord's power to come against specific evil spirits. Trust this discernment and support their prayers with your own prayers. If someone discerns a spirit of, say, anger, then understand that the prayers are directed not against the natural human emotion of anger but against an evil spirit which may have tempted you to sin through this human emotion or which may have so clouded your mind that anger is not functioning in your life correctly. (Anger, for example, is appropriate when directed against evil spirits. Anger becomes sinful depending on how it is used.) Prayers mentioning a "spirit of anger" are concerned with the demon which has manipulated anger in your life, not against you or the natural human emotion of anger in itself.

Step Two: Honesty

The second step in this approach is to instruct the person to be honest. In the various discussions which surround the prayers, the person should not misstate the truth in any way. He should try to be very exact, candid and straightforward, to speak the truth deliberately and consciously. He should decide to speak the truth, to renounce any intentions of coverup or deceit or of pride which would cause him to twist the situation so that it sounds better. For example, tell the person: if you have been experiencing temptations to steal, do not say, "God seems to have given me a taste for the good life, because I am strongly attracted to things." It is not shameful to admit temptations when appropriate. Bringing these temptations into the light will aid in the discernment process by the team.

This is not the same as encouraging people to tell their sins, and this distinction should be kept. Confession is not called for, but it is all right for them to mention occasions or patterns of temptation or demonic harassment. The goal is honesty, not revelations about personal sin. Those who are praying should keep special guard against any hint of curiosity or inappropriate interest in the person's private life. If the person prefers to consider these matters silently, that is allowable, yet it often helps to mention aloud the nature of oppressive temptations, without indicating whether the sin itself has been committed. In the end, of course, it is better for the person to be silent and honest with God than to speak aloud while being slightly dishonest.

STEP THREE: Confession and Renunciation
This third step is essential, especially if the pattern of temptation has been longstanding, or if certain sins have not been repented of. It is essential to be in right relationship with God before embarking upon prayers for deliverance.

The person should be told to bring to mind (but not to mention aloud) any serious sins by which he has turned away from God. (Note the different way of dealing with temptations, above.) The following specific sins should be mentioned by the leader: Satanism, the occult, marital infidelity, abortion, stealing or embezzlement, blasphemy, dishonoring the Lord, cursing others (distinct from profanity), refusal to believe Scripture or rightful spiritual authority. Others may be added by team members if their discernment so indicates.

If the person asks for clarification about any of these sins (Is a ouija board considered occult?), the leader should give clarification. (Yes, ouija boards have been used as avenues by evil spirits— perhaps not in your case, but you should renounce such things anyhow.)

The person should be encouraged to express contrition for serious sin, whether or not any sins have been mentioned aloud. He should renounce all the sins that the leader has mentioned. This act of renunciation is simply a declaration of personal rejection of such sins, a decision to have nothing to do with them, a commitment not to be mastered by Satan in these circumstances. Renunciation is not a prayer, but a statement of intent or a commitment. It does not imply that the person has ever in fact committed any of these sins. It is a good idea to instruct the person to renounce the sins *whether or not* he has ever committed any of them. This "covers all the bases" without infringing on the person's right to private confession. The person should speak aloud these renunciations, perhaps saying, "Lord, I renounce and oppose the evils of abortion, Satanism . . . and I thank you for saving me from my sins by Jesus' death on the cross. I want to stop the devil in his tracks and to prevent him from making further inroads into my life, in fact, to push him out of my life by your strength and grace." The person should be encouraged to make private renunciation of serious sins in addition to those mentioned aloud. (Catholics should be encouraged to resolve to receive the sacrament of Reconciliation.)

STEP FOUR: Forgiveness

The work of God in our lives can be impeded significantly when we are holding something against another person through a refusal to forgive. The leader should encourage the person to decide to forgive any such persons and to make efforts later to repair the relationships. Depending on the needs of the person, this time of praying in forgiveness might be protracted. The leader should be willing to take as much time as necessary to guide the person in the process of identifying people who should be forgiven. Perhaps it will be effective gradually to call to mind all the various stages of the person's life—childhood, teen years, etc.—as an aid in identifying areas of unforgiveness.

Caution the person against examining the motives or the background of the persons who have not been forgiven ("I don't think mom ever really loved me"). Rather, concentrate on specific hurts or incidents for which forgiveness has not been forthcoming. ("My father boasted about how well I was doing in school, but my grades were not very good. He expected more than I could give.")

It is important to consider hurts irrespective of whether they were inflicted intentionally. People have a hard time, sometimes, admitting that their parents did them wrong. At one level they hold a grudge but at another they need to believe their parents love them. For this reason forgiveness never takes place. Telling the person not to consider motives, etc., helps him face reality and enables forgiveness. Accidents, mistakes, confusion can also hurt and fester inside a person, even when the hurt was not deliberately inflicted. The important thing is to forgive the person for inflicting the hurt or for doing the harmful thing, not to determine whose fault it was. Parents, in particular, should be forgiven in this light.

The person should mention aloud the first names of the people if at all possible, providing confidentiality may be preserved. It is entirely possible that a major stronghold of Satan's power in the person's life will be broken at this stage of the session. The leader should not be too eager to rush on to the next steps. There will often be various emotional aspects to this stage—either an outrush of emotion (weeping, anger, despair) or a blockage of emotion (disinterest, depression, "I just can't remember anyone who's ever hurt me"). A pastoral sensitivity at this point is absolutely essential. The leader should be ready to help the person pray through whatever comes up. This step should close, perhaps, with a catch-all prayer forgiving "all those I just can't remember at all," and commending everything to God.

The team should be praying, discerning, bringing forth Scripture passages, words of encouragement and the like all through this time. Dependence on the gifts of the Holy Spirit is crucial throughout such sessions. The Holy Spirit will inspire those who are praying (and the person being prayed for) with invaluable directions and instructions in the process of praying. Openness to these inspirations can make short work of a process which otherwise could go on ineffectually for hours. The team should expect guidance from the Lord regarding the person's situation, events in the past, present circumstances, patterns of Satan's attack, specific temptations and in fact anything that may assist the prayer. God helps us as we pray. His intention is to minister to the person through his Christian brothers and sisters—this is the reason why a group has been convened rather than simply having the person pray by himself all alone. The body of Christ, gathered together, is alive in the power of the Holy Spirit, and thus can expect to be guided by the Spirit.

These inspirations should be discerned simply by describing them to the person or to the leader and asking whether they bring to mind a specific item which needs prayer, or whether they remind the person of a situation or a person which might have significance in the prayer of deliverance.

For example, one of the team might develop a strong sense from the Lord that the person needs to be reconciled to his brother. The team member should perhaps ask, "Do you have a brother?" and proceed to suggest that reconciliation may be called for. The person being prayed for may or may not see the importance of specific insights such as this one, but it is best to do at least a follow-up prayer in every case ("Lord, if there is any need for reconcilation with my brother, I promise to take care of it as soon as possible").

Sometimes the inspirations consist of an image of an object or of a symbolic scene, or other things which are open to numerous interpretations (a car out of control, a card game, a scepter on the ground). In such cases, after a clear description of the images, everyone should be encouraged to pray about what is signified. The leader should make the decision about how to proceed on this information, after consultation with the person being prayed for. One time, a team member saw a clear image of a tennis ball, which didn't mean anything until he mentioned it to the person being prayed for. It immediately brought to mind his longtime frustration at not being a good tennis player since his youth, and especially in matches with his cousin. This early experience of failure turned out to be an avenue through which Satan had cut away at the person's self-respect.

Openness to inspirations and the process of discernment should be a constant background of deliverance prayer.

STEP FIVE: An Act of Faith

Before praying with the person, the leader asks for an act of faith. The person should freely state his confident assurance that these prayers will be made in the name of Jesus Christ, trusting in his promise to listen to the prayers of his brothers and sisters. The person should lay claim in a deeply personal sense to the deliverance which is promised by God to those who follow Jesus Christ.

The person should express anticipation of this deliverance, a hopeful confidence in its accomplishment through the instrumentality of prayer. At this point the team should come forward with Scripture passages on this theme of faith in the promises of God (for example, Rom. 4:20-21, 1 Jn. 2:25-27, 2 Cor. 1:20).

STEP SIX: Praying for People

With so much to consider in the way of preliminaries and preparations, perhaps the actual occasion of prayer might seem anticlimactic. On the contrary, of course, the heart and soul, the major fruit of the prayer comes with the word of command and the direct invocation of the Lord and his powerful helps on behalf of the suffering person. This is also the aspect of the deliverance session which is least amenable to description or to advice at a distance. I could suggest specific formulas or rote prayers from Scripture or traditional sources—and these would have their effect—but it is also true that a spontaneous, unrehearsed time of prayer can allow the Holy Spirit to work in a powerful way different from his work through memorized prayers.

The aim is not originality, but openness to the Holy Spirit, who is the Adversary of whatever evil spirits may be involved with the person. We are like the sergeant in the midst of battle making a call to headquarters for an artillery strike on the enemy's position. Very simply, we call on God the Father, God the Son and God the Holy Spirit to actualize the freedom which Christ has already won from the snares and influences of the devil. The evil spirits are commanded to leave the person in question. The evil spirits are addressed directly, by name, as they become known through discernment. God is also addressed and asked to effect the liberation.

The words of command should closely follow the patterns set forth in Scripture. In general, the command is short, direct and to the point.

The leader, at least, must be comfortable with spontaneous prayer. Others involved in the session may prefer to recite memorized prayers such as the Our Father. If all participants in the session are members of the same denomination, they could make use of appropriate traditional prayers. Catholics, for example, could recite the Prayer to St. Michael the Archangel or invoke the assistance of Mary, the saints and the other angels on behalf of the afflicted person. Prayers from a variety of denominational traditions would also be appropriate, depending on the circumstances. Those who are praying should use whatever forms of prayer and intercession they are comfortable with. The leader should be free to answer the call of the Spirit directly, as discernment suggests. He can ask for God's help against specific evil spirits which are discerned to be present.

The leader should also be familiar with a large number of passages from Scripture, so that he can at the appropriate moment read or ask someone to read certain passages. I would suggest familiarity with at least Psalms 3, 8, 10, 11, 12, 13, 20, 22, 23, 31, 35, 54, 68 and 118. The Magnificat and the Benedictus (Lk. 1:46-56; 68-80) should also be included. The leader should also consider passages such as the prologue of John's Gospel (1:1-18), along with the various Gospel accounts of Jesus freeing people from the influence of demons, for example, Mark 1:32-35; 5:1-20; Luke 10:17-20; 11:14-22. Other passages should also be kept available for reference, such as Mark 5:25-34 (the healing of the woman with the flow of blood) and Mark 16:15-18 (the apostolic commission, "in my name they will cast out demons . . . "). Revelation 12:1-17 and 20:1-4, 7-11 are especially useful and effective.

It is wise to have the texts of traditional formulas and prayers available at any point during the prayer of deliverance. The leader should also be free to utilize whatever information has been gleaned in the preliminary stages to direct his intercessions specifically. For example, if certain temptations, tendencies, problems, past experiences or events have been mentioned in the times for renunciation, forgiveness, honesty and so on, then the leader can recapitulate these themes in direct prayer at this point.

Call upon the saving mercies of Christ, by the power of his death and resurrection. Declare God as the Lord of this person and of all evil spirits. Praise him and proclaim his authority throughout creation. Say or sing the psalms of triumph, of victory over enemies. Sing or recite hymns or songs of deliverance and thanksgiving. The prayer should in every sense be vibrant and alive, so even memorized prayers should be spoken with a greater intensity than might be normal or customary.

The person being prayed for should be encouraged to pray

also, in the same ways and with the same intensity and directness. Perhaps the leader can provide a prayer which the person repeats line by line after him, such as,

> God, my Father . . . Jesus, my Deliverer . . . Holy Spirit, my
> Purifier . . . I praise and thank you . . . for the power and
> the freedom from all evil influences . . . which you
> graciously and generously give to me. . . .
> I am your child . . . and I depend completely on you and on
> your strength. . . .
> I am not trusting in my own strength in this struggle . . .
> but in your unconquerable kingship and authority. . . .
> I have been attacked, Lord, . . . I have been under seige . . .
> and you are my only hope . . . .
> You are the One I trust in for deliverance. . . .
> I humbly ask, Lord, . . . that you cleanse me even from the
> desire for sin . . .
> so that I might cling closely to you . . . where there is eternal
> safety for me. . . .
> I reject Satan and I reject everything connected with that lying,
> evil creature. . . .
> I seek haven with you. . . . Your love for me will bring me
> through. . .
> although my enemies be many and powerful. . . .
> You are more powerful than all of them, Lord, . . .
> and you have come to help me.

If the influence of evil spirits can be pinpointed, then the prayers should bear down specifically upon that influence. In praying, it is best to be as definite and as specific as possible. "Get out, spirit of blasphemy."

Again, it is often useful to "cover all the bases." Even if no allusion to a certain evil influence (temptation to blasphemy, for instance) has been reported in the case history or in the session so far, members of the team may discern in prayer that it would be appropriate to pray against it or to command it to begone. This should be done in each case. It is not necessary to pray out loud (suggestibility may be a factor to consider), but the prayer should be made. It is good insurance. With such prayers, made by the leader, by the members of the team and the person being prayed for, the deliverance prayer draws to a close. The final prayers should be of thanksgiving for release.

If a second or third session has been planned, make sure the person has full information about the date, time, etc. Keep in close contact over the next few days to see what has happened. I think it is unwise to start this process of deliverance without providing for continued pastoral oversight and supervision. Otherwise, the devil who has been driven out may attack again with numerous additional spirits. This possibility has scriptural basis, as described in Matthew 12:43-45.

It is better to have multiple sessions scheduled in advance, since it might be disconcerting for the person to hear for the first time about a second session immediately after the first session. The person might be tempted to think that the first session somehow didn't work.

Though I have not emphasized it, love must be the foundation of the deliverance session. The Father's love for us, manifested in Jesus Christ, activated in us individually by the Holy Spirit, makes us agents of love for one another. The team members must have love for their afflicted brother or sister, because they, too, know what it is to suffer affliction, just as the Lord Jesus did. In everything, love must not fail.

Appendix I:
Catholic Pronouncements
on Satan's Activity

To summarize the official teaching of the Roman Catholic magisterium with respect to the demonic, we turn to council documents and official pronouncements. Most of the statements which the church has made about the devil are responses to and clarifications of distorted notions, rather than responses to doubts of the devil's existence. His existence is an assumption.

The church has on a number of occasions condemned the ideas that the devil is a sort of evil twin of God who was not created by God and is equal to him in power. For example, in 561 the Council of Braga (Portugal) stated,

> If anyone says that the devil was not first a good angel created by God, or that his nature was not the work of God, but that he emerged from darkness, and had no creator but is himself the principle and substance of evil, as Manes and Priscillian have said, *anathema sit* ("let him be accursed").[1]

The Fourth Lateran Council (1215) included this statement as part of its profession of faith:

> For the devil and the other demons were indeed created by God naturally good, but they became evil by their own doing. As for man, he sinned at the suggestion of the devil.[2]

Official church pronouncements also point out that one of the effects of original sin is to place men and women under the influence and power of the devil, and that one aspect of Jesus' saving mission is to free us from Satan's grasp. Thus the Council of Florence (1442) declared,

> [The church] firmly believes, professes and preaches that no one ever conceived from man and woman has been freed from the dominion of the devil except through faith in Jesus Christ our Lord. . . . With regard to children, on account of the danger of death which can often occur, since no other remedy can help them than the sacrament of baptism by which they are snatched away from the devil's dominion and made adopted sons of God, [the church] warns that holy baptism should not be delayed.[3]

Resist the Devil

The Council of Trent (1546) stated in its "Decree on Original Sin,"

> If anyone does not profess that Adam, the first man, by trans-
> gressing God's commandment in paradise, at once lost the holi-
> ness and justice in which he had been constituted; and that
> offending God by his sin, he drew upon himself the wrath and
> indignation of God and consequently death with which God had
> threatened him, and together with death captivity in the power of
> him who henceforth "has the power of death" (Heb. 2:14), i.e., the
> devil; and that "the whole Adam, body and soul, was changed for
> the worse through the offense of sin," *anathema sit*.[4]

Vatican Council II made this point in several documents. In the *Dogmatic
Constitution on the Church* (1964)[5] we find,

> But very often, deceived by the Evil One, men have become vain
> in their reasonings, have exchanged the truth of God for a lie and
> served the world rather than the Creator (see Rom. 1:21 and 25)
> (§ 16).

In the *Constitution on the Sacred Liturgy* (1963) the council taught,

> Accordingly, just as Christ was sent by the Father so also he sent
> the Apostles, filled with the Holy Spirit. This he did so that they
> might preach the gospel to every creature and proclaim that the
> Son of God by his death and resurrection had freed us from the
> power of Satan and from death, and brought us into the kingdom
> of his Father (§ 6).

In its chapter on doctrinal principles, the *Decree on the Church's Missionary
Activity* (1965) notes,

> However, in order to establish a relationship of peace and com-
> munion with himself, and in order to bring about brotherly union
> among men, and them sinners, God decided to enter into the
> history of mankind in a new and definitive manner, by sending
> his own Son in human flesh, so that through him he might snatch
> men from the power of darkness and of Satan (see Col. 1:13; Acts
> 10:38) and in him reconcile the world to himself (§ 3).

> [Missionary activity] purges of evil associations those elements of
> truth and grace which are found among peoples, and which are,
> as it were, a secret presence of God; and it restores them to Christ
> their source who overthrows the rule of the devil and limits the
> manifold malice of evil (§ 9).

Appendix I

The *Pastoral Constitution on the Church in the Modern World* (1965) says that the world

> . . . has been freed from the slavery of sin by Christ, who was crucified and rose again in order to break the stranglehold of the Evil One, so that it might be fashioned anew according to God's design and brought to its fulfillment (§ 2).

Farther on, in a chapter entitled, "The Dignity of the Human Person," the same document says,

> Although set by God in a state of rectitude, man, enticed by the Evil One, abused his freedom at the very start of history. . . . Man finds that he is unable of himself to overcome the assaults of evil successfully, so that everyone feels as though bound by chains. But the Lord himself came to free and strengthen man, renewing him inwardly and casting out the "prince of this world" (Jn. 12:31), who held him in the bondage of sin (§ 13).

The church has also, over the years, reminded Christians that the devil is the enemy of mankind and that Christian men and women must engage in spiritual combat with the devil and with demons. Thus, the Council of Florence called the devil "the enemy of the human race"[6] and the Council of Trent called him "the ancient serpent, the perpetual enemy of mankind."[7] The *Dogmatic Constitution on the Church* adds the following texts:

> We make it our aim, then, to please the Lord in all things (see 2 Cor. 5:9) and we put on the armor of God that we may be able to stand against the wiles of the devil and resist in the evil day (see Eph. 6:11-13) (§ 48).

> Let [the laity] not hide this their hope, then, in the depth of their hearts, but rather express it through the structure of their secular lives in continual conversion and in wrestling "against the world rulers of this darkness, against the spiritual forces of iniquity" (Eph. 6:12) (§ 35).

Also, we find the following statement in the *Pastoral Constitution on the Church in the Modern World*:

> The whole of man's history has been the story of dour combat with the powers of evil, stretching, so our Lord tells us, from the very dawn of history until the last day (§ 37).

It is only recently that the church has had to deal with the assertion that the devil and demons—indeed, the whole spiritual world—do not exist. In

1870, Vatican Council I proclaimed that God "made at once out of nothing both orders of creatures, the spiritual and the corporeal, that is, the angelic and the earthly."[8] In the encyclical *Humani Generis* (1950), Pope Pius XII listed a number of contemporary errors. Included in that list is this statement: "Some also question whether angels are personal beings, and whether matter and spirit differ essentially."[9]

Two more recent statements the church has made on the subject of the devil and demons reassert much of the past teaching and deserve to be quoted more extensively. The first of these is in the form of a talk Pope Paul VI gave in a general audience (November 15, 1972):

> What are the church's greatest needs at the present time? Don't be surprised at our answer and don't write it off as simplistic or even superstitious: one of the church's greatest needs is to be defended against the evil we call the Devil. . . . Evil is not merely an absence of something but an active force, a living, spiritual being that is perverted and that perverts others. . . . It is a departure from the picture provided by biblical and church teaching to refuse to acknowledge the Devil's existence . . . or to explain the Devil as a pseudoreality, a conceptual, fanciful personification of the unknown causes of our misfortunes. . . . St. Paul calls him the "god of this world," and warns us of the struggle we Christians must carry on in the dark, not only against one Devil, but against a frightening multiplicity of them. . . . So we know that this dark, disturbing being exists, and that he is still at work with his treacherous cunning; he is the hidden enemy who sows errors and misfortunes in human history. . . . He undermines man's moral equilibrium with his sophistry. He is the malign, clever seducer who knows how to make his way into us through the senses, the imagination and the libido, through utopian logic, or through disordered social contacts in the give and take of our activities, so that he can bring about in us deviations that are all the more harmful because they seem to conform to our physical or mental make-up, or to our profound, instinctive aspirations. . . .
>
> This matter of the Devil and of the influence he can exert on individuals as well as on communities, entire societies or events, is a very important chapter of Catholic doctrine which should be studied again, although it is given little attention today. Some think a sufficient compensation can be found in psychoanalytic and psychiatric studies or in spiritualistic experiences, which are unfortunately so widespread in some countries today.[10]

Appendix I

In 1975, the Sacred Congregation for the Doctrine of the Faith published *Les formes multiples de la superstition*, which it strongly recommended as a sure basis for grasping the teaching of the magisterium on Christian faith and demonology. Here we can see several important statements concerning the devil.

It would indeed be a fatal mistake to act as if history were already finished and redemption had achieved all its effects, so that it were no longer necessary to engage in the struggle [against the devil and demons] of which the New Testament and the masters of the spiritual life speak. . . . To maintain today, therefore, that Jesus' words about Satan express only a teaching borrowed from his culture and are unimportant for the faith of other believers is evidently to show little understanding either of the Master's character or of his age. If Jesus used this kind of language and, above all, if he translated it into practice during his ministry, it was because it expressed a doctrine that was to some extent essential to the idea and reality of the salvation he was bringing. . . . Satan, whom Jesus attacked with his exorcisms and confronted in the wilderness and in his passion, cannot be simply a product of the human ability to tell stories and personify ideas nor a stray survival of a primitive culture and its language. . . . Satan's action on man is admittedly interior but it is impossible to regard him as therefore simply a personification of sin and temptation . . . . It was for all these reasons that the Fathers of the church were convinced from Scripture that Satan and the demons are the enemies of man's redemption, and they did not fail to remind the faithful of their existence and action. . . . The assertion that demons exist and have power is not based solely on these more categorical documents. They find another, more general and less formal expression in conciliar statements every time the condition of man without Christ is described. . . . It was with this traditional teaching in mind that the Second Vatican Council, being more concerned with the present life of the church than with the doctrine of creation, did not fail to warn us against the activity of Satan and the demons. Vatican II, like the Councils of Florence and Trent before it, has once again proclaimed with the apostle that Christ came to "rescue" us "from the power of darkness. . . ." Elsewhere Vatican II renews the warning issued by the letter to the Ephesians that we must "put on the armor of God so that you may be able to stand firm against the tactics of the devil." For, as this same document reminds the laity, "our battle is not against human forces but against the principalities and powers, the rulers

of this world of darkness, the evil spirits in the regions above."
We are not surprised, finally, to see that, when the council wishes
to present the church as God's kingdom that has already begun,
it appeals to the miracles of Jesus and specifically to his exorcisms.
For, it was precisely with reference to exorcisms that Jesus made
the well-known statement: "The reign of God is upon you. . . ."
The liturgy directly echoes New Testament teaching when it
reminds us that the life of the baptized is a struggle, carried on
with the grace of Christ and the strength of his Spirit, against the
world, the flesh and the demonic beings. . . . To sum up: The
position of the Catholic Church on demons is clear and firm. The
existence of Satan and the demons has, indeed, never been the
object of an explicit affirmation by the magisterium but this is
because the question was never put in those terms. Heretics and
faithful alike, on the basis of Scripture, were in agreement on the
existence and chief misdeeds of Satan and his demons. For this
reason, when doubt is thrown these days on the reality of the devil
we must, as we observed earlier, look to the constant and universal faith of the church and to its chief source, the teaching of
Christ. It is in the teaching of the gospel and in the heart of the
faith as lived that the existence of the world of demons is revealed
as a dogma. The contemporary disaffection which we criticized
at the beginning of this essay is, therefore, not simply a challenge
to a secondary element of Christian thought but a direct denial of
the constant faith of the church, its way of conceiving redemption,
and (at the source of both of these) the very consciousness of Jesus
himself.[11]

The Catholic Church has always believed in the reality and
danger of the devil and of demons, and continues today to teach
and warn about them.

APPENDIX II:
CATHOLIC POLICIES
REGARDING EXORCISM

The Code of Canon Law reserves the public exorcism of possessed persons to the bishop and to his delegate, who must be a person of proven maturity, piety and moral integrity. All official written prayers or formulas used in the Roman Catholic sacramental of exorcism are reserved to official exorcists. These prayers may not be used without the authorization of the local bishop. Of course, any Christian can pray for God's aid against Satan at any time, and can also command Satan or any evil spirits to depart in the name and by the authority of Jesus. No one, however, should undertake a formal, public exorcism on his own authority.

Recently some Catholics and members of other denominations have conducted various seminars or workshops in which prayers of deliverance or exorcism are the chief spiritual objective. The dangers in such public procedures are readily apparent, and one can only express the hope that extreme caution be used in such situations. They are certainly not recommended in this book, and in fact we hope that the more pastorally and privately oriented methods described here take the place of these informal and sometimes dangerous practices.

In 1985 Cardinal Joseph Ratzinger of the Congregation for the Doctrine of the Faith issued some cautions for Catholics regarding informal exorcism sessions which were taking place at public gatherings. He asked bishops to make sure that only those with proper authority lead any such sessions, in which evil spirits were interrogated and cast out.

It is certainly true that the Lord chooses to work at such sessions, but we feel that the potential for scandal and harm to the person is disproportionately great.

Appendix III:
Case Histories

As an authorized exorcist in my Catholic diocese, I encountered only three genuine cases of what I believe to have been possession. By no means am I suggesting that this is the ordinary sort of experience a Christian should expect when praying for deliverance. Quite the contrary. As I note elsewhere, in cases where possession is suspected, an appointed exorcist must be contacted.

Case 1

This young man (C.) was referred to us by a local agency to whom he had recourse for help after he found himself compulsively driven to commit suicide. He had slashed his wrists and, later, "coming to himself," realized what he had done and sought help.

My first impression, as he spoke of bizarre visions and voices, was that C. needed psychiatric intervention. However, when he talked on subjects other than the demonic he seemed quite normal and intelligent. He had been a Methodist and started to study for the ministry, got involved with drugs and the occult and had made a pact with Satan to seduce women. In this he had been very successful.

I agreed, after hearing his story, to pray with the team for him and gave him some holy water with which to sprinkle his room. I told him to repent of his past, to read the Bible and to pray. At our first session we prayed for two hours. He seemed to experience some inner struggle and to hear voices say, "We are not coming out." I do not think we were convinced that this was a case of the demonic, although we were impressed by his sincerity and normality. The following week was an extremely difficult one for him. He was harassed by visions and voices; sleep was troubled by nocturnal noises and shaking of the bed.

At the second prayer session he became quite violent and would have assaulted me as the leader had not two men forcibly restrained him. During the prayers his face was frequently quite contorted and he snarled and hissed. The use of holy water, prayer in tongues and particularly the invocation of St. Michael the Archangel provoked severe reactions. After this session, in our team consultation we were convinced that we were dealing with evil spirits. On our team was a member of the Mental Health

Clinic whose psychiatric experience was very helpful in analyzing the situation.

At the third session some spirits were identified: spirit of mockery, spirit of deceit, spirit of lust, Satan. Because of my position as a Catholic exorcist, I began all sessions with exorcism prayers from the *Roman Ritual*. As it became clear that numerous evil forces were present, we forbade them to communicate with one another in order to deal with them one by one.

With each session the reaction to the prayers of exorcism was less violent. C. was urged to renounce the various spirits himself and to command them to leave. The final session was the most dramatic. The spirit of lust was forced to leave and then Satan. When Satan left, the chapel was filled with the odor of sulfur dioxide. I did not notice it myself since a tremendous concentration is required of the one leading the exorcisms, but the other five did and opened the door for fresh air.

This young man, 24 at the time, went on to go through a Life in the Spirit Seminar and to be baptized in the Holy Spirit. He became quite active in prayer groups, was married, and both he and his wife are now very active in church ministry.

Case 2

Our second case history concerns a man of middle age who was recommended by a priest to our ministry. This man gave the following personal history:

> My problem began one night in the second or third week of January, 1952. I was riding in a small, one-person compartment (of the type popular at that time) on an express passenger train traveling between Chicago, Illinois, and Los Angeles, California. On the first night of the journey, as I was getting into bed, I turned out the lights and, to my considerable amazement, saw a luminous gray cloud hovering over the bed. I immediately turned the lights back on and could then no longer see the cloud. By snapping the lights off and on, I determined that the object could only be seen in the dark. Then, upon turning the lights off once more, the object could be seen diving for my body into the area of the solar plexus. This was accompanied by the most acute sense of terror that I have ever experienced before or since.
>
> The cloud seemed to be trying to penetrate the body, and I believe it succeeded. However, the struggle took the entire night. As the sun rose in the morning, the feeling of wildly extreme terror suddenly stopped, but I remained quite shaken.
>
> The next day, as I reflected on what had happened, I decided that I must have gone mad. That began my search for some

psychological explanation. Also, a rather severe anxiety remained.

A few months later, during a physical examination, it was discovered that I had cancer of the thyroid. The surgeon who performed the subsequent operations told me that, had the cancer not been found when it was, I would have had two more years to live.

However, the anxiety problem which had begun on the train was in no way diminished. Also, I began having very bizarre dreams, and experienced a few rather alarming extrasensory-type phenomena.

I obtained both psychiatric and psychological counseling and read many psychology books myself. Many years of this procedure produced zero results.

In 1973, I took up a study of yoga in the hopes of calming my nerves in this way. This led to the reading of occult literature in general. During this period the extrasensory phenomenon greatly accelerated, and so did the anxiety!

In May, 1976, while living in Arizona, I experienced a massive escalation of the problem. I was inundated with both visual and auditory phenomena of a most sinister kind. As the origin of the problem now, for the first time, seemed obvious, I purchased a crucifix which I wore around my neck. On the second day that I had the crucifix, I was sitting in my apartment reading a book with the crucifix hanging on the outside of my shirt. I happened to glance down at the crucifix and saw a very distinct double image. There was a second crucifix superimposed over the first. As I looked, invisible hands seemed to take the legs of the second image of Christ, and violently tear the body in half. This was accompanied by a burst of hate and rage so palpable that it seemed to fill the entire room and bounce off the walls.

After that, things got continually worse. I consulted two Protestant ministers, who obviously didn't believe me.

Since 1977 I have traveled all over the country, and some foreign countries as well, seeking help. The majority of Catholic priests I have consulted do not believe in the existence of evil spirits, and one even insisted that there is no such thing as evil! The others simply don't know what to do about it.

We asked the person to keep a diary of what was being experienced after a prayer session. I give excerpts from this diary.

Thursday, June 28: Less than usual harassment during the day. At prayer time there was *no* interference! On the very rare occasions in the past when there was no interference with prayer, the following night was usually worse than usual. This night was no exception. At 2:00 a.m. I awoke from a nightmare in which I had dreamed that I was peacefully lying on a bed (oddly, the bed didn't look like any I can remember actually sleeping on) when a demon creature dived at me out of the air and began strangling me.

Later, I dreamed that hostile strangers walked into my house and drove me out.

Shortly after this I noticed that I was feeling quite nauseous. Later, I developed diarrhea, which tapered off by afternoon. When the diarrhea began, a mocking spirit voice sang, "doing what we know best."

Friday, June 29: Less than usual harassment, but still some feeling of nausea. At prayer time the voices sounded very distant and could hardly be heard.

Sunday, July 1: Very soon after I awoke in the morning harassment began and lasted all day. The voices sounded quite angry, and I believe they were trying to make up for their missed harassment time the previous day.

Monday, July 2: I was quite tired and slept most of the day. Fortunately, there were no nightmares at this time and very minimal harassment the rest of the day. However, after being asleep for about four hours that night, a rather lengthy nightmare occurred. It was of the accusatory type. I can remember at least three things in the same dream that I was alleged to be guilty of: I was accused of being a dope addict, a pornography addict and a murderer. Most of my dreams can be classified as being one or the other of only two types. In the one type I have my good name destroyed by lies, and in the other type there is depicted physical violence against me. Sometimes the attempted murders are depicted quite graphically.

Wednesday, July 4: Very angry voices when I mowed the lawn, and considerable interference with my writing of checks in payment for bills later in the day. Any constructive activity is always strongly opposed. Sabotage at prayer time was determined and continuous. Twice the normal time was required to pray through the interference.

Three hours after going to sleep, I was awakened by viciously evil-sounding voices. They kept repeating death threats. Then one said, "We are going to have a *double* sacrifice!" It didn't say who the other half of the sacrifice was supposed to be.

After some praying, the voices stopped and I went back to sleep. About two hours later a different set of voices woke me and began angry scolding. Although there were no nightmares I got very little sleep.

Thursday, July 5: Alternating periods of silence and angry scolding. I was able to take a two-and-a-half-hour nap during the afternoon. Only average harassment at prayer, and no nightmares.

Friday, July 6: A very bad day. Vicious hate talk and crazy talk most of the day. A bad headache in the evening, and very persistent sabotage from the voices at prayer time. One nightmare and awakened several times by noise.

In ensuing conversations we learned this man was living alone with only a cat for company. He had no friends and he avoided people because of his "affliction" lest they should be scared or fail to understand. His "spirits" also resented anything that created happiness. He had an income which was quite sufficient for his needs and did not need to work beyond the concern for his investments. We urged him to engage in some physical activities (his only exercise was daily to walk the cat), and to become involved in some works of charity. Clearly he was deeply introverted and we felt his symptoms might diminish if he developed some activities that would take him out of himself. At least, this should be tried. He found excuses not to follow any suggestions we made. We finally concluded that his problem was basically psychological. Our conclusion was based on the facts (1) that there was no response to the prayers, (2) that he was unwilling to accept suggestions "to get out of himself," (3) that he was well acquainted with occult literature and knew all the symptoms.

When we gently intimated our conclusion, he was quite indignant and declared he would search for someone with better discernment.

CASE 3

S. was a middle-aged woman referred to us by her family. She had been in a mental institution several times but declared "they" did not understand her. She was a very religiously oriented woman with holy pictures and statues in her home. She read many spiritual books, said the rosary daily, and was subject to great harassment in prayer. Voices would forbid her to go to Mass or to receive the Eucharist. At times she would throw things at the statues or rip her rosary apart, later to be filled with great compunction for what she had done. We began the prayers of exorcism, to which she seemed to respond appropriately, repelling the crucifix, etc. She was on medication which created a dry mouth and would

Appendix III

ask for a drink when we were praying with her. On one occasion I told one of the team to pour a little holy water in the glass before giving it to her. She took one swallow and exploded it over the team and surroundings.

On reviewing the session afterward, the team was puzzled: something about the reactions was not authentic. I suggested that the next time she asked for a drink, a little holy water be poured into the glass in such a way that she would not observe it. This time she drank the water very calmly. In the course of our sessions we became aware through our conversations with her that she had read a number of things on "possession." We concluded that she was unconsciously imitating what she had read and that our ministry could not help her.

I do not wish to imply that these people in the last two cases are insincere. They are disturbed. They believe what they are saying, which is of the essence of delusion; they are afraid of the demonic and of what they are experiencing. Yet, at the same time, they are finding some satisfaction in it.

People whom we have judged truly possessed, on the contrary, wonder in their "normal" state whether what is happening is real, whether they are deluded, whether they need psychiatric care. This expression of possible psychiatric assistance being necessary is a straw in the wind, if one is dealing with people who are emotionally and psychologically well-balanced. One is inclined to suspect demonic activity when they become concerned about their mental or emotional balance. Normal people would tend to find a natural explanation for the phenomena.

CASE 4

Another lady was referred to us by a prayer group in another city. She had been "seeing things" for many years. When her daughter began "seeing things" she decided to do something about it. In the past she had given herself to Satan to win a man she was in love with. Among the things she "sees" is a man to whom she feels in bondage and who plays sexual games with her.

After several sessions she revealed that she had been on medication but now refused to take it. We urged her to return to the medication and she refused. Consequently, we terminated the sessions. (If a person refuses to follow reasonable suggestions, we ordinarily terminate prayer, reasoning that deliverance will take place only if the person wants to be freed and, hence, will follow suggestions.) Our conclusion was that the daughter was "seeing things" due to suggestion because the mother was. The woman was living in a fantasy world with the man whose love she had tried to win–a situation reinforced by psychological instability. Her prayer group continued to pray with her and to urge her to resume medication.

Eventually she did so, the "visions" disappeared, and she is living a normal life. Was this due to the prayer and support she received or to the medication or to both? God only knows.

In some of the cases I have described, it will be noticed that the deciding factor in the discernment only surfaces after several sessions of prayer. The team prays and discerns. Bits of history are revealed gradually. Prayer, discernment, consultation with the team eventually lead to a reasonable awareness of the source of the trouble.

It is not impossible that joined with these abnormal psychological states of the last two cases is some demonic activity which is thereby disguised. One may *quietly* pray for the well-being of such persons without intimating demonic activity to them. In their state, any confirmation of their supposed demonic obsession will only make matters worse.

Appendix IV:

Bibliography

The Comedy of Dante Alighieri: Florentine, tr., Dorothy Sayers, *Cantica II, "Il Purgatorio"* (Baltimore: Penguin Books, 1955).

Deliverance from Evil Spirits: A Weapon for Spiritual Warfare, Randy Cirner and Michael Scanlan (Ann Arbor: Servant Books, 1980).

Demon Possession, John W. Montgomery (Minneapolis: Bethany House Publishers, 1976).

The Devil: Does He Exist and What Does He Do?, Albert Delaporte, translated from the sixth French edition, revised and corrected (New York: D. & J. Sadlier & Co., 1890).

Dictionnaire de spiritualite: ascetique et mystique, doctrine et histoire, vol. III,*"Discernement des esprits,"* Joseph Pegon (Paris: Beauchesne, 1952), pp. 1222-1291.

Love and Will, Rollo May (New York: Norton, 1969).

Les maladies nerveuses ou mentales et les manifestations diaboliques, J. de Tonquedec (Paris, 1893).

The Seven Deadly Sins Today, Henry Fairlie (Notre Dame: University of Notre Dame Press, 1979), reprint of the edition published by New Republic Books, Washington.

Soundings in Satanism, F.J. Sheed (New York: Sheed & Ward, 1972).

Spiritual Warfare: Defeating Satan in the Christian Life, Michael Harper (South Plainfield: Bridge Publishing Company, 1970).

Whatever Became of Sin?, Karl Menninger (New York: Hawthorn Books, 1973).

NOTES

1. One interesting case study is King Saul, who is moved to jealousy, rage, hatred and terror by evil spirits and does not hesitate to engage in necromancy (1 Sam. 16:14-23, 18:10-16, 19:8-10, 28:4-25). See also such passages as Leviticus 16:8-26, Isaiah 51:9, 27:1, and 1 Chronicles 21:1.

2. Ernest Russier, "Satan," *Catholic Mind* (Sept., 1974), LXXII: 1285, pp. 13-25.

3. Quoted in F.J. Sheed, *Soundings in Satanism* (New York: Sheed & Ward, 1972), p. 120.

4. Justin Martyr, "Second Apology," tr. Thomas B. Fall, in *The Fathers of the Church*, ed. Ludwig Schopp (New York: Christian Heritage, Inc., 1948) pp. 125-126.

5. Irenaeus, *Against Heretics* II, 32, 4.

6. Lactantius, *Divine Institutes* IV, 27.

7. Minucius Felix, *Octavius*, 27.

8. St. Ambrose, *Letter to Marcellina* 22, 2. The laying on of hands mentioned by Ambrose was to exorcise those possessed by evil spirits.

9. Tertullian, *To Scapula*, tr. Rev. S. Thelwall, in *The Ante-Nicene Fathers*, vol. 3, ed. Rev. Alexander Roberts and James Donaldson (New York: Charles Scribner's Sons, 1925), p. 107.

10. Origen, *Against Celsus* VII, 67.

11. E.H. Gifford, *St. Cyril of Jerusalem and St. Gregory Nazianzen* (*Library of Nicene and Post-Nicene Fathers*, second series, VII; London, 1984); p. xix.

12. *Clementine Homilies*, III, 13.

13. Cyril, *Procatechesis*, XIII, 14.

14. See Gifford, *Cyril*, pp. xix-xx.

15. Cyprian, *Letter to Magnus*, 75, 16.

16. Ignatius of Antioch, *Letter to the Ephesians*, 13.

17. St. Augustine, *De Symbolo ad Catechumenos*, I, 2.

18. Augustine, Letter 194 (To Sixtus).

19. Augustine, *Contra Julianum*, III, 3, 8.

20. Mandate XI, 1, 8-17.

21. *Testaments of the Twelve Patriarchs*, IV, 14-16.

22. *Procatechesis* XIV, quoted by Gifford, *Cyril*, p. xx.

23. Tertullian, *Apologetics*, XXIII.

Notes

24. Justin Martyr, *Dialogue with Trypho*, 85.

25. Origen, *Against Celsus*, I, 6.

26. Justin Martyr, *Dialogue with Trypho*, 76, 6.

27. Gifford, *Cyril*, p. xix.

28. Pseudo-Clement, "First Letter to the Virgins," 12.

29. *Apostolic Constitutions*, VIII 3, 26.

30. *Ecclesiastical History*, VI, 43.

31. Epistles of Cyprian, 74, 10.

32. Council of Antioch in Encaeniis, Canon X.

33. Synod of Laodicea, Canon XXVI.

34. *Roman Ritual*, X.

35. Origen, *Against Celsus*, I, 9.

36. Louis Monden, *Signs and Wonders: A Study of the Miraculous Element in Religion*, (New York: Desclee & Co., 1966), p. 140.

37. Tertullian, *De Spectaculis*, XXVI. Note that the Roman theater of which Tertullian speaks was often obscene, orgiastic, violent, cruel. Here, as he mentions, the cry "To the lions!" was raised against Christians.

38. Justin, *First Apology*, XIV.

39. Rollo May, *Love and Will*, p. 129.

40. Ibid., p. 103.

41. M.F. Unger, *Demons in the World Today*, p. 102.

42. Augustine, *De Genesi ad Litteram*, XIII, 14—XIV, 1.

43. *Shepherd of Hermas*, 14.

44. Henry Fairlie, *The Seven Deadly Sins Today* (Notre Dame: University of Notre Dame Press, 1979), p. 17.

45. G.K. Chesterton, *All Is Grist*.

46. Dante, *The Comedy of Dante Alighieri: Florentine*, tr. Dorothy L. Sayers (Baltimore: Penguin Books, 1955), p. 188.

47. John of the Cross, "The Dark Night" I, 7, in *The Collected Works of St. John of the Cross*, tr. Kieran Kavanaugh and Otilio Rodriguez (Washington, D.C.: ICS Publications, 1979), pp. 310-311.

48. Sayers, quoted in Fairlie, *Seven Deadly Sins*, p. 114.

49. Sayers, *Dante*, p. 209.

50. John of the Cross, "Dark Night" I, 3.

51. Sayers, *Dante*, p. 219.

52. John of the Cross, "Dark Night" I, 6.

53. See C.S. Lewis, *The Four Loves* (London: Geoffrey Bles, 1960), p. 109.

54. Ibid., p. 111.

55. Quoted in Fairlie, *Seven Deadly Sins*, p. 178.

56. Ibid., p. 177.

57. Ibid.

58. John of the Cross, "Dark Night" I, 4.

NOTES TO THE APPENDICES

1. *The Christian Faith in the Doctrinal Documents of the Catholic Church,* rev. edition ed. J. Neuner, S.J., and J. Dupuis, S.J. (New York: Alba House, 1982), p. 119.

2. Ibid., "Chapter 1: On the Catholic Faith," pp. 14-15.

3. Ibid., "Decree for the Jacobites," p. 392.

4. Ibid., pp. 137-138.

5. *Vatican Council II: The Conciliar and Post Conciliar Documents,* ed. Austin Flannery, O.P. (Northport, New York: Costello Publishing Company, 1975). All further references to the documents of the Second Vatican Council are from this source.

6. *The Christian Faith,* "Decree for the Jacobites," p. 178.

7. Ibid., "Decree on Original Sin," p. 137.

8. Ibid., "Dogmatic Constitution on the Catholic Faith," p. 124.

9. National Catholic Welfare Conference translation, printed by the Daughters of St. Paul, Boston.

10. *The Pope Speaks,* Vol. XVII, No. 4 (Washington, D.C.: TPS Publications, winter, 1973), pp. 315-318.

11. *Vatican Council II: More Postconciliar Documents,* ed. Austin Flannery, O.P. (Northport, New York: Costello Publishing Company, 1982), pp. 456-485.

More books from Greenlawn Press to build your faith!

Jesus Lives Today!

By Rev. Emiliano Tardif, M.S.C.

Share the excitement of God's miraculous power in our time! *Jesus Lives Today!*, which has sold over half a million copies worldwide in 14 languages, gives you the testimony of a priest whose own healing led him from skepticism about miracles to full involvement in an international healing-prayer ministry. Its wealth of documented healings and conversions, as well as the prayers throughout the book for God's grace and power, show you what God can do when people humbly give him full control.

Order # GRNL913X, $6.95, paperback

Mighty in Spirit

By Joseph Bagiackas

You gain a fresh, modern perspective on the seven gifts of the Holy Spirit by reading *Mighty in Spirit*. This very helpful book deals with Christian character and charismatic spirituality. Its use of Scripture passages, traditional wisdom and personal testimonies shows you how the Spirit's gifts can enrich your daily life.

Order # GRNL8004G, $2.45, saddle-stitched

Open the Windows—The Popes and Charismatic Renewal

Edited with an introduction by Rev. Kilian McDonnell, O.S.B.

Open the Windows is the first book to gather in English translation all the major statements and documents of Popes Paul VI and John Paul II on the Catholic charismatic renewal. You learn how the popes have welcomed and pastored this movement. Fr. McDonnell gives you informative introductions to each document.

Order # GRNL9067, $5.95, paperback

(Please turn to next page!)

God Is at Work in You:
A Practical Guide to Growth in the Spirit
By Ralph Rath
If you want to grow in daily zeal for the Lord, *God Is at Work in You*
is perfect, whether you have just come to know the Lord or have been
leading a strong Christian life for some time. You receive Scripture
readings, real-life examples and reflection questions in each chapter.
Inspiration and advice are yours regarding daily prayer, discerning
God's will, sharing the gospel, and more. Prayer-group leaders—and
others in pastoral ministry—can find solid teaching material here!
Order # GRNL9113, $4.95 paperback

Order these books today from your local Christian bookstore
or directly from:

Greenlawn Press
Dept. R
107 S. Greenlawn Ave.
South Bend, IN 46617
(Please add $1.50 to total order for shipping and handling.)